HOW TO WRITE
DAZZLING DIALOGUE

THE FASTEST WAY TO IMPROVE ANY
MANUSCRIPT

JAMES SCOTT BELL

Published by Compendium Press

CONTENTS

1

THE FASTEST WAY TO IMPROVE ANY MANUSCRIPT

You are an editor or agent looking over a pile of fiction proposals. You've poured your coffee, you issue a big sigh, and look at the first project of the day. You skip the cover letter and synopsis. This saves you time. For if the writing is terrible, or even mediocre, you don't have to bother with the rest. The cold, hard reality of manuscript submissions is that after all the work on the query letter and all the stress of trying to perfect a synopsis, it's the first couple of pages of the sample chapters that will likely determine the fate of the author.

So let's say you look at project number one, and it goes something like this:

CHAPTER ONE

Monica sat on the park bench and looked at the bustling activity before her. Boys and girls played in the sandbox.

A man was throwing a Frisbee to his dog. The dog ran fast across the green grass and jumped into the air, catching the whirling disc in its mouth. Oh, the joy of that dog. If only Monica could recapture some of that exuberance!

How long had it been since Richard had left? Two years? She should have been over it by now. But her life alone had taken on a sameness and a safety, and perhaps that was as it should be. There was a hole in her heart that only Richard could fill. Hole? No, a wound.

When she was eight years old, Monica had set her heart on owning a show pony. She saw it one day at a horse show in town. Her father had taken her there as a reward for...

Let me ask, do you care about what the reward was for? Hasn't the narrative, slow to begin with, now ground to a halt with a visit to the past?

But the main problem I see is what I call the "character alone, thinking" opening. It's all too common in manuscripts from new writers.

So you toss that proposal aside and pick up the next one.

CHAPTER ONE

"I simply will not have it!" Robert Massingale expostulated. "Not while I am the head of this family of five. Goodness knows it is hard enough to run an estate during the reign of Her Majesty, Queen Victoria. But having a servant from Hungary come into this house without the proper references, and with a scar across his left cheek to boot, which he no doubt got in a waterfront bar somewhere during his thirty years on this earth, I tell you, I simply will not have it."

"Of course," Janet Massingale, his wife of thirty-three years, agreed. "You always know best."

"Thank you, my dear," said Robert gratefully. "Shall I ring for tea?"

"Do, yes, and please have Caldwell, our butler, serve it in the library. I do so enjoy looking out at our estate, which is far enough away from London that we may consider ourselves country folk."

Egad! Bloated, expository dialogue. No two people in the real world would talk to each other that way. It's clear the writer is trying to slip information to the reader, and doing it ham-fistedly.

You pass on that one. It's beginning to look like a very long day. Maybe you'll stop here and play some Fruit Ninja while you finish your coffee.

But no, you've got to make a dent in this pile, so with another sigh you take up proposal number three. And here is what you see:

CHAPTER ONE

"Any thoughts that you'd like to start with?"

"Thoughts on what?"

"Well, on anything. On the incident."

"Oh, the incident. Yes, I have some thoughts."

She waited but he didn't continue. He had decided before he even got to Chinatown that this would be the way he would be. He'd make her have to pull every single word out of him.

"Could you share them with me, Detective?" she finally asked. "That is the purpose of—"

You stop mid-sentence. This has more promise than the other two you've read. It's because the dialogue is crisp and tense.

Which means you are *immediately* more confident that this writer knows what he's doing. So you pause and check out the author's name. Michael Connelly. Hmm. The book is titled *The Last Coyote*.

You go back to the chapter, and the dialogue continues to shine.

Which is why you read on.

Dazzling dialogue has done its job.

But what if you don't want to be an agent or editor in this hypothetical? Maybe you've decided to go into self-publishing, and all you care about are readers.

The same dialogue dynamics apply. Readers react just like the industry pros, only on a subconscious level. Great dialogue increases their confidence in the author. That, in turn, makes it more likely they'll finish your book.

On the other hand, flabby dialogue will dull the motivation to read on.

Which kind of makes dialogue important, don't you think?

Indeed, I believe dialogue is the fastest way to assess the skill of a writer of fiction.

This means it's also the fastest way to improve your manuscript.

And that's why I've written this book.

When I was first learning the craft of fiction I did not find much helpful material out there on dialogue. Since I was writing screenplays at the time, I had to figure out that part, and fast, because scripts are virtually all about characters talking to each other. So I read a ton of screenplays and novels, taking special note of the dialogue.

I took notes on what I learned, came up with some techniques and tools, and applied them to my own fiction. Some years later, after I was a published author, I began to teach these techniques in my workshops on the fiction craft.

That material is now presented in this book.

Let's start with a definition of fictional dialogue. What it is ... and what it isn't!

WHAT DIALOGUE IS ... AND ISN'T

One day I was sitting happily in Starbucks, doing some reading, when the bane of civilized society plunked down at a table nearby. I am referring to the ubiquitous loud-and-obnoxious phone talker (or *loud-ob* for short).

You know what I mean (and I hope you're not one of them!) They put the phone to their ear and think they have to kick up their voice several decibels in order for the other party to hear them. Every word they utter breaks the sound barrier of social etiquette, and lays waste to any hope of calm reflection by the neighboring victims.

Further, this particular loud-ob was the worst variety—the kind who does most of the talking, and keeps it up as if the conversation were a marathon. This loud-ob seemed like she could yak for a week. And, as far as I could tell, she was talking about absolutely nothing of consequence.

Luckily I had my noise-canceling headphones and iPod with me. But before piping some smooth jazz into my ears, I took a moment to type up some of the stuff she was saying:

"Okay, listen, I think he knows about me, but, you know, what I'm saying is, to him, is that you have a hard time doing what's right, what you do is so other worldly, and Megan needs to hear it, the very thing that you're dreading is in an odd way the thing you need. Does that make sense?"

Um, no, I wanted to shout. *So you don't need to go on!*

Okay, maybe to the loud-ob phone talker it made sense, but not to anyone else. And that means we have here an instance of what fictional dialogue is *not.* The talk that comes out of your characters' mouths must always have a purpose. Yes, sometimes that purpose might be to blather, but only because such blathering is a way for the character to accomplish something. More on that below.

What Dialogue Is

The definition of dialogue I like best comes from a well-known playwright and screenwriter named John Howard Lawson (blacklisted, I might add, during the McCarthy era). In his book, *Theory and Technique of Playwriting,* Lawson states that dramatic dialogue should always be "a compression and extension of action."

Speaking, Lawson explains, "comes from energy and not from inertia." Thus, dramatic speech "serves, as it does in life, to broaden the scope of action; it organizes and extends what people do. It also intensifies the action. The emotion which people feel in a situation grows out of their sense of its scope and meaning."

If you think of speech as action, it will keep you from writing soggy, inert dialogue. Speech as action reminds you that characters talk in fiction because they want to further their own ends.

But what if my character is into small talk? What if my character is just killing time?

Then you have to know *why* she is killing time.

Is she nervous about something? Hiding a secret? Trying to avoid the truth?

It has to be *something*, or the dialogue is just taking up space.

Every word, every phrase that comes out of a character's mouth is uttered because the character hopes it will further a purpose.

The character has, in short, an *agenda*.

When I was on a board of directors once, we had an officer who ran great meetings. The first thing he did when he sat down at the table was to ask for an "agenda check." He'd take suggestions, decide which items were relevant and then place them in priority order. This always kept the meeting from being a grand waste of time.

So the first secret of dazzling dialogue is to give your characters their own agenda checks in every scene.

Then, put those agendas in opposition.

Suppose you were writing a novel about a spoiled Southern belle just before the start of the Civil War. In this story, the belle (let's call her Pansy) has her heart set on marrying a certain gentleman.

One problem. It has just been announced that this gentleman is going to marry someone else. Now Pansy must act quickly or lose her true love forever.

She formulates a plan. There's a big barbecue coming

up at the gentleman's ancestral home. Pansy decides to get him alone and force him to declare his love for her.

That's how Margaret Mitchell set up *Gone With the Wind*. (She also had the good sense to rename her character Scarlett).

And so we come to the barbecue scene. Scarlett gets her ideal man, Ashley Wilkes, into the library. What then? She talks. She uses her words as an extension and compression of action. She has an agenda. She's not subtle about it. She blurts it right out. "I love you!"

Now, what is Ashley's agenda? As a southern gentleman with impeccable manners and a code of conduct, he must stop this sort of talk in its tracks. He does love Scarlett, but cannot say so or allow himself to dwell on it. So he tries light-hearted banter. "Isn't it enough that you've already collected every other man's heart here today?"

But Scarlett does not back down. "Ashley—Ashley—tell me—you must—oh, don't tease me now! Have I your heart? Oh, my dear, I lo—"

Ashley disrupts the outburst by putting his hand on her mouth. Now the contest begins in earnest. Here is the dialogue from that scene, without any of the narrative parts:

"You must not say those things, Scarlett! You mustn't. You don't mean them. You'll hate yourself for saying them, and you'll hate me for hearing them!"

"I couldn't ever hate you. I tell you I love you and I know you must care about me because—Ashley, do you care—you do, don't you?"

"Yes, I care ... Scarlett, can't we go away and forget we have ever said these things?"

"No, I can't. What do you mean? Don't you want to—to marry me?"

"I'm going to marry Melanie. Father is to announce the engagement tonight. We are to be married soon. I should have told you, but I thought you knew. I thought everyone knew—had known for years. I never dreamed that you—you've so many beaux, I thought Stuart—"

"But you just said you cared for me."

"My dear, must you make me say things that will hurt you?"

Scarlett continues to use words to try to convince him her love is better than Melanie's. When he doesn't bite, she switches tactics.

"I shall hate you till I die!"

When that doesn't get the job done, she stops talking, deciding that instead of a compression and extension of action, she'll use *real* action. She slaps Ashley across the face.

Ashley walks out of the room.

Scarlett, in a fit of pique, throws a porcelain bowl against a marble mantelpiece. A man's voice says, "This is too much."

It's that rogue from Charleston, Rhett Butler! And he was lying on the sofa, unseen, as her scene with Ashley unfolded.

"It is bad enough to have an afternoon nap disturbed by

such a passage as I've been forced to hear, but why should my life be endangered?"

"Sir, you should have made known your presence."

"Indeed? But you were the intruder ..."

"Sir, you are no gentleman."

"An apt observation. And you, Miss, are no lady."

The character of Rhett Butler brings a different agenda to the scene, one of gentle mockery. He wants to knock Scarlett off her high horse. She, of course, wishes to stay there.

This is the first and most important lesson in dazzling dialogue: be clear on every character's agenda in a scene, and set the agendas in conflict. Before you write take just a moment to jot down what each character in the scene wants, even if (as Kurt Vonnegut once said) it is only a glass of water.

What Dialogue Isn't

Dialogue is not real-life speech. It is *stylized* speech for which the author, through the characters, has a purpose.

That's a crucial distinction. We don't want to merely capture reality in our fiction. We aren't filming a documentary.

What we do is render something that *feels* real but is intended to create a desired effect.

Real-life speech is meandering and often boring.

Fictional speech doesn't meander (unless, of course, a character has a strong reason to run on and on).

Dialogue is not the information superhighway. It's not to be used as a lazy way to give the reader information or a sermon on the author's view of the world. There are ways to do this, as you'll see further on in this book, that are unobtrusive.

So that's the foundation for dazzling dialogue. It comes from a character who has an agenda, and is directed toward another character who has an agenda. No matter how small or large the objectives, if they are in conflict the dialogue will work. Let me show you with a short clip from one of the great dialogue movies of all time, *All About Eve* (1950). This is the story of Margo Channing (played by Bette Davis), an aging Broadway diva, and her young charge, Eve Harrington (Anne Baxter). Prominent in the film is the narrator, the nasty, witty and all-powerful critic, Addison DeWitt (George Sanders, in an Oscar-winning role).

In an early scene, Margo is throwing a party in her spacious New York apartment. She has been angry at DeWitt for subtly hinting that she is a bit too old for the roles she's been playing. Thus, between the two of them, there's a snarky power struggle.

DeWitt has with him a comely young woman named Miss Caswell (played in the film by Marilyn Monroe at her most Marilyn-ish). Regarding Miss Caswell, DeWitt's agenda is to not be too embarrassed to be seen with her. She is on his arm because he's bedding her in return for doing her theatrical favors, like introducing her to famous producers. Here at the party, DeWitt doesn't want Miss Caswell to come off as too much of an airhead, lest his reputation as a social maven suffer.

Miss Caswell's agenda is to ingratiate herself with the others, unaware that she sticks her foot in her mouth with virtually every line.

And what is Eve's agenda? Ah, I shall not spoil the movie by telling you all about Eve. Perhaps you can begin to discern her agenda in the following:

MARGO
(to Addison)
I distinctly remember striking your name from the guest list. What are you doing here?

ADDISON
Dear Margo. You were an unforgettable Peter Pan - you must play it again, soon. You remember Miss Caswell?

MARGO
I do not. How do you do?

MISS CASWELL
We never met. That's why.

ADDISON
Miss Caswell is an actress. A graduate of Copacabana School of Dramatic Arts.

(his glance is attracted
by Eve coming downstairs)
Ah ... Eve.

EVE

Good evening, Mr. DeWitt.

MARGO

I had no idea you knew each other.

ADDISON

This must be, at long last, our
formal introduction. Until now we
have met only in passing ...

MISS CASWELL

That's how you met me. In passing.

MARGO

Eve, this is an old friend of Mr.
DeWitt's mother - Miss Caswell,
Miss Harrington. Addison, I've been
wanting you to meet Eve for the longest time.

ADDISON

It could only have been your
natural timidity that kept you from
mentioning it.

MARGO
You've heard of her great interest
in the theater?

ADDISON
We have that in common.

MARGO
Then you two must have a long talk.

EVE
I'm afraid Mr. DeWitt would find me
boring before too long.

MISS CASWELL
You won't bore him, honey. You
won't even get to talk.

ADDISON
My dear, come closer.
(Miss Caswell does, and he points)

There is Max Fabian. He is a
producer. Go do yourself some good.

MISS CASWELL
Why do they always look like
unhappy rabbits?

ADDISON
Because that is what they are. Now go
and make him happy.

The great script by Joseph L. Mankiewicz works throughout because all of the characters, every one of them, is after something. And they are situated so that they may each be in conflict with the others at any time.

This is the big secret of dazzling dialogue.

But there's a whole lot more you can do to make it shine.

STORY WEAVING: THE TRUE ART OF DIALOGUE

Dialogue in fiction has five functions. One or more of the following must always be at work, or you're just taking up space:

1. Reveal story information
2. Reveal character
3. Set the tone
4. Set the scene
5. Reveal theme

1. Reveal Story Information

Exposition is necessary in fiction (though not as much as many writers think!) What we mean by exposition is information that is necessary for the reader to understand what's going on in the story.

There are two ways to deliver this information: through narrative or through dialogue.

Narrative is sometimes employed because it's best to get the information out of the way and move on with the story. Like this:

Frank was a box boy at Gelson's, where he'd worked for ten years.

Another way to do it is to put the information within narrative that is reflecting the character's inner life:

Frank hated being a box boy at Gelson's. Ten lousy years of this drudgery.

Dialogue is sometimes the more artful way to reveal story information. But here's the key: the reader must never catch you simply feeding them exposition!

Here's what I mean. I see this type of dialogue in beginning manuscripts all the time. One character talking to another character, but a little bit of info is slipped to the reader in a clunky fashion, as in, "Hello, Arthur, my family doctor from Baltimore. Come on in to my house on Mockingbird Lane."

Here, information both of the characters *already know* is spouted, something that destroys the illusion of reality. I made the example obvious for illustrative purposes. So here is another example. This is from the opening of an episode from the old *Perry Mason* television show, which ran in the late 1950s through the early '60s. In those days, expositional dialogue was often used to set up the hour-long dramas. In this episode, a man and woman are standing in a train compartment. The train is not yet moving.

HARRIET
I still wish I were going to Mexico with you instead of staying here in Los Angeles.

LAWRENCE
This trip's going to be too dangerous, Harriet. It's some of the most rugged terrain in the Sierra Madre mountains. It's no place for a woman, especially my wife. It's almost no place for an amateur archaeologist, either. Thanks for coming with me as far as Cole Grove station.

You see what's happening? It's the writers shooting information to the viewers through expository dialogue.

The first thing to look out for is a character saying anything that both the characters already know. In the above example, they both know they live in Los Angeles. They both know she's his wife. They both know he's an amateur archaeologist. They both know he's going into the Sierra Madre mountains. And they both know they're going as far as Cole Grove station.

Again, we understand why it was done within the confines of a one-hour TV drama from the '50s. But you're writing a novel.

At a conference where I was teaching once, a student turned in a manuscript with the following (used by permission). A woman (Betty) has been planting bombs to avenge the death of her son. She now has a forensic investigator (Kate, who has been closing in on her) tied up, and is threatening to kill her:

Betty looked down at Kate. The triumphant smile on her

face faded into a snarl at the mention of her son's death. "Why do you care?"

"Because if my son had died as a result of finding out about something terrible that had happened to him that I had kept hidden to protect him, I would want to blame the person responsible." Kate thought she would try the empathy tactic. She did feel a great sorrow for Betty and her tragic story. She watched as Betty returned her statement with a hard stare.

Here in this tense moment, Kate has revealed to Betty facts about the case, but the dialogue sounds unnatural. The long line has information stuffed into it, but it feels like it's for the reader's benefit rather than the character's.

I told the student to go back and cut all dialogue that is not absolutely true to the character and the emotional beats. What would either of them really say?

So what's the right way to handle expositional dialogue?

First, determine just how much exposition you really need. Especially toward the front of your novel. Here's one of my axioms: *Act first, explain later.* Readers will wait a long time for explanatory material if there is solid action going on.

In fact, by not revealing the reasons behind certain actions and dialogue, you create mystery. That works in any genre. Readers love to be left wondering.

Second, once you know what you need to reveal, put it into a *tense* dialogue exchange.

In other words, *hide the exposition within confrontation.*

Let's say you have former lovers meeting at their 30th

high school reunion. A less careful writer might do it this way:

> He saw Sylvia across the room. His cheeks heated up. After that night at the cabin, he had never called her again. He'd avoided her at school. He would practically run from her if he saw her in the hall.
>
> She had not come to the first two reunions, much to his relief. But now here she was, coming toward him.
>
> "Hello, Sam," she said.
>
> "Hi, Sylvia," he said. "Nice to see you again."

That's fine. It works. It gets the information across. But what if it happened this way?

> Sam felt a tap on his shoulder and turned around.
>
> "Hello, Sam."
>
> His mouth fell open.
>
> "Cat got your tongue?"
>
> "Sylvia."
>
> "Aren't you going to give me a hug?"
>
> "What? Oh, sure."
>
> He gave her a hug and felt like he was holding a block of ice.
>
> "There, isn't that better now," Sylvia said.
>
> "Better?"
>
> "Why didn't you call me?"
>
> "Oh, jeez, Sylvia—"
>
> "Why are your cheeks pink, Sam? Something you want to tell me? I know! You can tell me why you didn't call."

A ton of information has been delivered here. You can supplement the dialogue with actions and inner thoughts. The reader doesn't need to get all the information at the beginning. In fact, it creates more discomfort if they don't know all of what's going on.

Orrie Hitt was a paperback original writer from the '50s and '60s, who wrote what were politely called "steamy potboilers." But he knew his craft. Here is some exposition. In his novel, *Add Flesh to the Fire,* a man's ex-wife returns to him, but he wants nothing to do with her. She has just offered herself to him physically:

"What you came here for, baby, you could pick up in any bar."

"Shut up."

"I won't shut up. What do you think I am? Nuts? You run off with my own brother, get a divorce, he was better than I was, you said, and two years later you show up. You want me to roll out the red carpet? You want me to stand on my head?"

"I don't blame you for being bitter."

"Bitter doesn't describe it."

She tried to reach up and touch my face but I jerked my head aside.

Another type of exposition relates to plot points. Why, for example, is everyone after the black bird in Dashiell Hammett's *The Maltese Falcon*? One of the characters, Casper Gutman, explains:

"Mr. Spade, have you any conception of how much money can be made out of that black bird?"

"No."

The fat man leaned forward again and put a bloated pink hand on the arm of Spade's chair. "Well, sir, if I told you—by god, if I told you half!—you'd call me a liar."

Spade smiled. "No," he said, "not even if I thought it. But if you won't take the risk just tell me what it is and I'll figure out the profits."

The fat man laughed. "You couldn't do it, sir. Nobody could do it that hadn't had a world of experience with things of that sort, and"—he paused impressively—"there aren't any other things of that sort." His bulbs jostled one another as he laughed again. He stopped laughing, abruptly. His fleshy lips hung open as laughter had left them. He stared at Spade with an intentness that suggested myopia. He asked; "You mean you don't know what it is?" Amazement took the throatiness out of his voice.

Spade made a careless gesture with his cigar. "Oh, hell," he said lightly, "I know what it's supposed to look like. I know the value in life you people put on it. I don't know what it is."

Notice what Hammett does here. He uses dialogue to convey the value of the black bird, but not in one big lump. He doles it out in a conversation that has breaks, self-interruptions and actions. That way, the dialogue and the scene itself never seem static.

A few pages later, Gutman tells the whole story of the Maltese Falcon, in what is essentially a speech. Hammett uses new paragraphs virtually without interruption. The key there is that the information itself is interesting! So if you have a character make a speech, make sure he isn't a bore.

2. Reveal Character

Here's another exchange from *The Maltese Falcon*, where the hard-bitten gumshoe, Sam Spade, is paid a visit in his office by Joel Cairo, a "small-boned dark man of medium height ... The fragrance of *chypre* with him."

"Sit down, Mr. Cairo."

Cairo bowed elaborately over his hat, said, "I thank you," in a high-pitched thin voice and sat down. He sat down primly, crossing his ankles, placing his hat on his knees, and began to draw off his yellow gloves.

Spade rocked back in his chair and asked: "Now what can I do for you, Mr. Cairo?"...

"May a stranger offer condolences for your partner's unfortunate death?"

"Thanks."

"May I ask, Mr. Spade, if there was, as the newspapers inferred, a certain—ah—relationship between that unfortunate happening and the death a little later of the man Thursby?"

Spade said nothing in a blank-faced definite way.

Cairo rose and bowed. "I beg your pardon." He sat down and placed his hands side by side, palms down, on the corner of the desk. "More than idle curiosity made me ask that, Mr. Spade. I am trying to recover an—ah—

ornament that has been—shall we say?—mislaid. I thought, and hoped, you could assist me."

Spade nodded with eyebrows lifted to indicate attentiveness.

We can tell a lot about these two characters just from the dialogue. Who talks like Cairo? Someone of "breeding" and a certain air of snobbishness.

Spade, on the other hand, says exactly one word when the conversation gets going. The other times he reacts in silence.

Character can also be revealed through relationships. Charles Lederer wrote the screenplay for the Howard Hawks classic, *His Girl Friday* (1940). The movie was based on a famous play, *The Front Page* (1928) by Ben Hecht and Charles MacArthur. Hecht has long been considered one of the great dialogue masters. The play is about a newspaper reporter, Hildy Johnson, and his editor, Walter Burns. Burns wants to keep Hildy on the paper because he's such a great reporter. Hildy is going to quit the business to get married.

The brilliant move of the film was to turn Hildy into a woman who was once married to Burns. Notice in the following exchange how much we learn about the characters. Some of it is by action, such as when Burns doesn't light Hildy's cigarette, as a gentleman would, but tosses her matches.

The details about their relationship come through dialogue that is not angry, but is subtly tense. Each character is vying for advantage.

HILDY
May I have a cigarette, please?

(Burns reaches into his pocket, extracts a cigarette and tosses it on the desk. Hildy reaches for it.)

HILDY
Thanks. A match?

(Burns delves into pockets again, comes up with matchbox, tosses it to Hildy, who catches it deftly, and strikes the match.)

BURNS
How long is it?

(Hildy finishes lighting her cigarette, takes a puff, and fans out the match.)

HILDY
How long is what?

BURNS
You know what. How long since we've seen each other?

HILDY
Let's see. I was in Reno six weeks -- then Bermuda ... Oh, about four months, I guess. Seems like yesterday to me.

BURNS
Maybe it was yesterday. Been seeing me in your dreams?

HILDY

No — Mama doesn't dream about you any more, Walter.
You wouldn't know the old girl now.

BURNS

Oh, yes I would. I'd know you any time–

BURNS AND HILDY

— any place, anywhere —

HILDY

You're repeating yourself! That's the speech you made the
night you proposed. "— any time — any place —
anywhere!"

BURNS

I notice you still remember it.

HILDY

I'll always remember it. If I hadn't remembered it, I wouldn't
have divorced you.

BURNS

You know, Hildy, I sort of wish you hadn't done it.

HILDY

Done what?

BURNS

Divorced me. It sort of makes a fellow lose faith in himself.
It almost gives him a feeling he wasn't wanted.

HILDY
Holy mackerel! Look, Walter, that's what divorces are for.

BURNS
Nonsense. You've got the old-fashioned idea that divorces are something that last forever — till 'death us do part'. Why, a divorce doesn't mean anything today. It's only a few words mumbled over you by a judge. We've got something between us nothing can change.

HILDY
I suppose that's true in a way. I am fond of you, Walter. I often wish you weren't such a stinker.

BURNS
Now, that's a nice thing to say.

HILDY
Well, why did you promise me you wouldn't fight the divorce and then try and gum up the whole works?

BURNS
Well, I meant to let you go — but, you know, you never miss the water till the well runs dry.

When revealing character through dialogue, consider:

Vocabulary

What is the educational background of your characters?

What words would they know that correspond to that background?

What if you have a character of limited education attempting to use "big words" to build himself up? This is also an indicator of character. Or it may be that the character is striving, in all good conscience, to better his station in life.

The point is, consider vocabulary as one aspect to deepen your own understanding of character.

Syntax

When a character does not speak English as a first language, syntax (the order of words) is the best way to indicate that.

For example, a newly arrived Bosnian might say, "Can you tell me please where is bathroom?"

Syntax can also be part of a character's attempt to speak in a heightened way. Our old friend Joel Cairo, in *The Maltese Falcon*, says, "No, no. Our private conversations have not been such that I am anxious to continue them. Forgive me for speaking so bluntly, but it is the truth."

Regionalisms

Do you know what part of the country your character comes from? How do they talk there?

I'm from L.A., and I still can't figure out what "supper" is. But people from Mississippi seem to have no problem with that.

Peer Groups

Groups that band together around a specialty—law, medicine, surfing, skateboarding—have pet phrases they toss around. These are great additions to authenticity. The best way to find them is to interview people from such a group, and just ask them!

3. Set the Tone

The kind of book you're writing is evident from the way people in your story talk to each other. Can you tell that the following are from different genres?

"I say, Doris, shall we be taking luncheon on the terrace or in the drawing room?"

"I prefer the terrace. The view of the garden is so lovely this time of year."

"Back off, sister, unless you want a belly full of lead."

"I do love you, Ross, I do. But I can't disappoint Frank."

"What I give you Frank can never give you. What we have, you and Frank can never have."

"Please, don't."

"I reckon we'd better go into town."

"I reckon you're right."

"Reckon we'll find some trouble?"

"I reckon we will."

"Good, because this is a day of reckoning."

You get the idea. The cumulative effect of dialogue on readers sets a tone for your book. Be intentional about what you want that tone to be.

4. Set the Scene

Dialogue can also help readers experience being in the scene.

First, the way characters react to their surroundings tells us both about the location and the people reacting to it.

"Man, this place is creepy. What's with all the hanging vines?"

"I hate San Francisco! I hate all the hills and the fog and the superior attitudes!"

Second, the dynamics of the scene can often best be set up through dialogue. Instead of this:

Once I was in the interview room, Agent Hofstra asked me to sit down. I gave him some lip, but he was totally in control of the situation. He gave me a veiled threat. I decided to sit down.

Try this:

"Sit down," Agent Hofstra said.
    "Don't feel like it," I said.

"You're not on the street anymore. In here you do what I tell you."

"I got a sore butt."

"That's not all that's gonna be sore. You see this little room we're in? You see any cameras? Recording devices?"

I decided to sit down.

5. Reveal Theme

"If you want to send a message, try Western Union." So said the film mogul Samuel Goldwyn. He knew that audiences want a story first and foremost. They do not want a lecture or a sermon.

Certainly, many writers do care about message, or theme. The danger in dialogue is to allow the characters to become mere mouthpieces for the message. This is called getting "preachy."

The way to avoid this is to place the theme into natural dialogue that is part of a confrontational moment. As with exposition, a tense exchange "hides" what you're doing. I lay out a method for accomplishing this later, in the section called "Thematic Dialogue."

Now that you know the purposes of dialogue in fiction, let's turn to training your ear for it.

4

TRAINING FOR DIALOGUE

They didn't fool around in ancient Sparta.

The boys all went into the military—at age seven. They spent the next ten years in rigorous training and education in the art of soldiering. Daily they'd be wrestling, boxing, throwing javelins and generally getting their bodies subjected to the toughest conditions.

The women in Spartan society were also taught physical resilience. You never knew when you'd have to spear some Athenian trying to take over your tent.

No wonder nobody wanted to fight the Spartans.

The lesson for writers is, learn to wrestle and throw spears.

And also train your ear for dialogue.

Below are some exercises that will help you do just that.

The Voice Journal

One of my favorite exercises when planning a novel is the Voice Journal. This is a free-form document, stream of consciousness, in the character's own voice.

How do I know what the character's voice sounds like? I prompt them with questions and then let them talk. I do this fast, without thinking about it much. What I'm waiting for is the moment when the character starts talking to me in a voice I did not plan.

And it always happens. That's the fun part, when the character starts to take on life for me.

We don't want our characters sounding the same when they speak, and the Voice Journal helps you avoid that condition.

Here's an example from my Voice Journal for a character in a story I'm working on:

So yeah, I been a cop fourteen years, and they get to you after a while. So you put on a screen, an act, you deal with it. My wife couldn't deal with it, so she left, we're still friends and all, but I got a little girl I only see every other weekend. That's crap. But I figure she's better off with her mother.

I go sometimes to the skating rink and I don't even skate. Never could. My ankles always turned in, my dad'd laugh at me for that. So I laugh at other people all the time. It takes the edge off. They don't know I'm laughing, so what harm does it do? Guy fell down the steps at City Hall the other day. Homeless guy, one of those, you know? Down he goes, right in front of a bunch of people. Some woman goes over to help him.

Me, I laughed.

Take your time with this journal. Don't try to do it all in one sitting. I come back to it often with my main characters, adding to it, analyzing it, sharpening it.

For your supporting cast, you can make the journals a little shorter. The key is to get to a place where each character who is going to talk in your novel has his or her own distinct pattern of speech.

Out Loud

You get an entirely different take on your dialogue when you read it out loud. Your mind "hears" it as if from the outside.

The other thing you can do is have your writing program (e.g., Word) "read" the text to you. Again, you get a fresh take.

This exercise will sharpen and expand your "ear" for dialogue.

Convert Movie Scripts

Another great practice for fictional dialogue is to read a movie script and convert the scenes into narrative form. (You can find several legit sources for movie scripts online, such as www.imsdb.com.)

Screenplays are mostly dialogue, mixed with a little bit

of direction. Take those elements and re-write them as fiction.

Then step back and look at the dialogue. Does it work the same? What can you change to make it more effective?

Here, for example, is a section from the Paul Newman movie *Cool Hand Luke*. It's the first time the ruthless Captain faces the new prisoner, Luke Jackson.

CAPTAIN
     Lucas Jackson.

LUKE
     Here, Captain.

CAPTAIN
     Maliciously destroyin' municipal
     property while under the influence.
     What was that?

LUKE
     Cuttin' the heads off parkin' meters,
     Captain.

CAPTAIN
     Well, we ain't never had one of them.
     Where'd you think that was gonna get
     you?

LUKE
     I guess you could say I wasn't
     thinkin', Captain.

CAPTAIN
>(looking at record)
>Says here you done real good in the
>war: Silver Star, Bronze Star, couple
>Purple Hearts. Sergeant! Little time
>in stockades. Come out the same way
>you went in: Buck Private.

LUKE
>That's right, Captain. Just passin'
>the time.

Now let's turn that into book prose. Add whatever you wish to make a scene.

"Lucas Jackson?" the Captain said.

"Here, Captain," Luke said.

The Captain stepped in front of Luke, looked up at him. Luke could smell the Brylcreem on the little man's head. The Captain glanced at the file.

"Maliciously destroyin' municipal property while under the influence. What was that?"

"Cuttin' the head off parkin' meters, Captain."

A half smile crept across the Captain's face. "Well, we ain't never had one of them." The Captain turned to the guy they called Boss Paul, who smiled and shook his head.

When he turned back to Luke, the Captain's eyes seemed beadier somehow.

"Where'd you think that was gonna get you?" he said.

Luke tried to size him up. He'd been able to judge the

cut of a man's jib ever since he was eight years old and working in his daddy's bar. And when a man with power tried to put you back on your heels, you had to push back. When that man had real power, the power to take some flesh off your bones, you had to make the push gentle at first.

"I guess you could say I wasn't thinkin', Captain," Luke said.

Luke kept his gaze steady as the Captain studied him.

The little man looked at Luke's record again. "Says here you done real good in the war."

Luke said nothing.

"Silver Star, Bronze Star, couple Purple Hearts." He paused, his eyes widening. "Sergeant! Little time in stockades. Come out the same way you went in, Buck Private."

"That's right, Captain," Luke said. "Just passin' the time."

Yes, this is work, but so is becoming a better fiction writer. The more you exercise your dialogue muscles, the better it will be on your own pages.

Improvisation

When I was an out-of-work actor (a role I specialized in) I took classes. My favorite exercise was improvisation. It forced me to think on my feet and be as creative as possible on the fly.

It also got me into character instantly and speaking like a completely different person.

So if you want another venue for training your voice, take an improv class from a local community college or theater group. It's fun, it exercises your imagination and who knows? Maybe you'll be offered a sitcom.

A "down and dirty" way to do improv, however, is right in your own home. Watch TV with the sound off, and do the voices of the characters. I find it best to do this with commercials. The ads move fast, so you have to.

This may sound silly or crazy, but guess what? You're a writer. You're already crazy. Go ahead and grease that wheel.

Here is another exercise: Below is a list of 28 stock characters grabbed from a Wikipedia list. Using a random number generator, once a day pick a character and stand up and start talking like that character. Man or woman, it doesn't matter. Just be the character. [NOTE: This is best done in your home and not, oh, Starbucks. Though if it's a Starbucks in Hollywood no one will probably notice.]

It's fun. For five minutes, walk around and be this character, talking like you think this character would talk. Comment on life, the universe and everything.

Don't think. Just do. It doesn't matter how accurate you are. What you are doing is stretching your mind. Believe me, when you start writing dialogue, your mind will be much more limber in coming up with a unique sound.

Here's the list:

1. Absent-minded professor
2. Action hero
3. Alien invader
4. Bad boy

5. Boy next door

6. Girl next door

7. Cat lady

8. Dark Lady (femme fatale)

9. Holmesian detective

10. Hardboiled detective

11. Elderly martial arts master

12. Farmer's daughter

13. Gentle giant

14. Gentleman thief

15. Geek

16. Grande dame

17. Jock (athlete)

18. Mad scientist

19. Outlaw

20. School diva

21. Southern belle

22. Space pirate

23. Tomboy

24. Town bully

25. Town drunk

26. Tycoon

27. Wise old man

28. Zombie

Just Practice

Write lots of dialogue for practice. Set up scenes with two random characters. Make them as different as possible.

Or observe two people in public and write a scene with what you think those characters might be saying to each other. Make them distinct voices. Give them conflicting agendas.

Do all these things and pretty soon you'll notice a vast improvement in your ability to write dialogue. And you know who else will notice? Agents, editors and readers.

And they'll be even further drawn to your story when you ratchet up the conflict and tension in the dialogue scenes. That's the subject of the next chapter.

5

INCREASING CONFLICT AND TENSION IN DIALOGUE

If dialogue is the fastest way to improve a manuscript, then the fastest way to improve your dialogue is to amp up the conflict and tension.

The dullest exchanges are those between two people on the same wavelength, with nothing gripping to talk about. I call these "sitting-down-for-coffee scenes." Watch out for them. If you do have two friends or allies sitting down to talk, don't make it just about feeding the reader information. Make some trouble. Here's how.

Remember Those Agendas

This is an all-too-typical scene early in a cop novel:

"Whatta we got here?"
"Looks like he took two to the heart."
"What was it?"
"Probably nine mil auto."

"Uh-huh. Anybody see it?"

"We talked to two people from the bar, said they heard the shots."

"How many?"

"Two. Auto fire."

"Good work."

"Thank you, sir."

This does the job of conveying information, but without tension or conflict. What if we added clear and differing agendas? What if the second detective didn't want the first to take over the investigation?

"Whatta we got here?"

"What's it look like?"

"Looks like gunshot to the heart."

"Thanks for stopping by."

"Anybody see it?"

"I got it covered."

"That's not what I asked."

Already there is more interest here. And all it took was adding objectives in conflict.

As I mentioned earlier in this book, figure out each character's desire in each scene and shape them so they face some form of opposition from the other characters.

Get Into More Arguments

Of course, if the agendas create sparks that lead to flames, so much the better. Arguments can run the gamut from mild disagreement to outright screaming matches. That gives you a wide berth, and a simple rule for scenes that seem to drag: just get the characters into an argument. Even a playful argument will work. Consider this from Nick and Nora Charles of Dashiell Hammett's *The Thin Man*. This is the opening of a chapter:

Nora said: "You just showing off, that's all it is. And what for? I know bullets bounce off you. You don't have to prove it to me."

"It's not going to hurt me to get up."

"And it's not going to hurt you to stay in bed at least one day. The doctor said—"

"If he knew anything he'd cure his own snuffles." I sat up and put my feet on the floor. Asta tickled them with her tongue.

Nora brought me slippers and robe. "All right, hard guy, get up and bleed on the rugs."

I stood up cautiously and seemed to be all right as long as I went easy with my left arm and kept out of the way of Asta's front feet.

"Be reasonable," I said. "I didn't want to get mixed up with these people—still don't—but a fat lot of good that's doing me. Well, I can't just wander out of it. I've got to see."

"Let's go away," she suggested. "Let's go to Bermuda or Havana for a week or two, or back to the Coast."

"I'd still have to tell the police some kind of story about that gun. And suppose it turns out to be the gun she was killed with? If they don't know already they're finding out."

"Do you really think it is?"

"That's guessing. We'll go there for dinner tonight and—"

"We'll do nothing of the kind. Have you gone completely nuts? If you want to see anybody, have them come here."

Set Up Barriers

Another way to add tension is to erect a barrier to communication. These can be outer or inner barriers.

For example, if two people are discussing a deep, dark secret that must be dealt with immediately, the intrusion of another character at just the wrong moment adds an outer barrier:

"She's his daughter?" Mary said, her voice dropping to a whisper.

"Not only that," said Rachel. "She's his sister."

"We have to ...we must—"

"Hello, girls!" It was Hedy LaRue, the new hire from the office. She pulled up a chair and sat down. "I have the greatest news to tell you!"

"Um, Hedy," Rachel said, "this isn't really—"

"I'm going to get married!" Hedy said.

And while we're on the subject of outer barriers, let's talk about interruptions. In fiction, you show an interruption by use of the em-dash followed by a close quote. No period or other punctuation. (When a character's voice trails off, use the ellipsis ...) See the passage in the last section, the argument between Nick and Nora Charles.

Sprinkle interruptions into your dialogue.

Dialogue tension can also be increased by interior barriers. Most often this is because one character has an emotional reason for not talking, or avoiding a subject. Usually this is something the other character is unaware of.

Suppose two lifelong friends are sitting down at Starbucks. Gasp! A sitting-down-for-coffee scene! If you're not careful, it could end up like this:

"So, Rachel, how have you been?"
   "Great, thanks. Feeling good."
   "You look good. Who's doing your hair now?"
   "Julie Milton at Blue Waters."
   "Oh, I love that place."
   "It's a cute place, isn't it?"
   "Very cute."

Communication isn't difficult here, is it? So let's put up a barrier. Let's suppose that one of them has a reason not to be so open with her friend. Out in the parking lot, just before coming in, her friend's husband whispered an indecent proposal in her ear:

"So, Rachel, how have you been?"
   "Fine, fine."
   "You look good. Who's doing your hair now?"
   "My hair?"
   "You know that stuff all over your head?"
   "Ah. Julie."

"Julie ..."

"Milton. Julie Milton."

"You okay, Rach?"

"What?"

"You sound a little distant."

"I'm fine."

"Honey, if there's something—"

"Let's talk about you. How are things with Joe?"

"Never better. He's been so sweet lately." Tamara took a sip of coffee. "Rach, truly, is something wrong?"

Now I want to read this scene. I want to know if the secret's going to come out or if Rachel will be able to resist. I want to know if they'll still be friends when the scene is over. Conflict and tension are doing their work.

Any scene in your book can have added conflict.

There's a great little scene in the screwball comedy classic *The Awful Truth* (1937). Jerry (Cary Grant) and Lucy (Irene Dunne) play a wealthy New York couple. When each suspects the other of having an affair they decide to get a divorce.

Lucy calls their lawyer. He's an older gentleman in a fine home. He comes into his library from the dining room to answer the phone:

Lawyer: Hello? Hello, Lucy! What's that? Divorce? You and Jerry? Now, now Lucy, don't do anything in haste that you might regret later. Marriage is a beautiful thing, and you should give it every—

At this point, the man's wife marches in and interrupts.

Wife: Why can't they call you back after we've finished eating?

Lawyer: (covering the phone with his hand) Please be quiet, will you? (Back on phone) You seem agitated, Lucy. Try and calm yourself. I hate to see you take any hasty action in a matter like this. Marriage is a beautiful thing—

Wife: Why don't you finish your meal? Why can't they call you back later?

Lawyer: (covering phone) Will you shut your mouth? (Back on phone) As I was saying, Lucy, marriage is a beautiful thing, and when you've been married as long as I have, you'll appreciate it, too.

Wife: Your food is getting ice cold. You're always complaining about your food. How you—

Lawyer: Will you shut your big mouth. I'll eat when I'm good and ready if you don't like it you know what you can do, so shut up! (Back on phone) Lucy darling, marriage is a beautiful thing.

What was a simple little phone call scene turned into a comedy gem because of the bump up in conflict.

Try this: Select a scene in your manuscript that doesn't seem as strong as it should be. Take each character in the scene and bump up the conflict between them by 25%. Find a way to do it. Add an annoying quirk, or interruptions, or a more scathing remark. Get the fire going then stoke the flames.

Dialogue full of conflict and tension is also the fastest way to improve your scenes.

The Fear Factor

I like to ponder the concept of fear when I'm working on a scene. The great thing about fear is that it is a continuum. On one side is simple worry, the fear that you have forgotten something, for example. On the other side is outright terror. In between is a whole range of emotion. At any given time, every character in a scene can be fearful about something.

In the coffee scene above, Rachel is obviously worried about whether to tell Tamara that Joe just came on to her. We can flesh out that worry some more.

Is Rachel worried about the friendship? Is she worried Tamara might not believe her?

What if she knows Tamara once had a breakdown over Joe's dalliances?

Or maybe she's attracted to Joe and doesn't want Tamara to find out.

What about on Tamara's side? What if she's so concerned with her image she's fearful that her friends might find out her marriage is in trouble?

Work on the fear factor from various angles. You will find that it's almost magical how your dialogue in that scene improves.

Here, for example, is a scene from Charles Webb's novel, *The Graduate*. This of course became the basis of the famous movie starring Dustin Hoffman and Anne Bancroft.

In this scene, young Benjamin Braddock has decided to start an affair with Mrs. Robinson. He must therefore secure a room at a hotel. But inside he is full of fear that he'll be found out, that the desk clerk will know exactly what's going on.

The fear factor and all the attendant tension come out beautifully in a scene that is almost all dialogue:

"Yes sir?" the clerk said.

"A room. I'd like a room, please."

"A single room or a double room," the clerk said.

"A single," Benjamin said. "Just for myself, please."

The clerk pushed the large book across the counter at him. "Will you sign the register, please?" There was a pen on the counter beside the book. Benjamin picked it up and quickly wrote down his name. Then he stopped and continued to stare at the name he had written as the clerk slowly pulled the register back to his side.

"Is anything wrong, sir?"

"What? No. Nothing."

"Very good, sir," the clerk said." We have a single room on the fifth floor. Twelve dollars. Would that be suitable?"

"Yes," Benjamin said, nodding. "That would be suitable." He reached for his wallet.

"You can pay when you check out, sir."

"Oh," Benjamin said. "Right. Excuse me."

The clerk's hand went under the counter and brought up a key. "Do you have any luggage?" he said.

"What?"

"Do you have any luggage?"

"Luggage?" Benjamin said. "Yes. Yes I do."

"Where is it?"

"What?"

"Where is your luggage?"

"Well it's in the car," Benjamin said. He pointed across the lobby. "It's out there in the car."

"Very good, sir," the clerk said. He held the key up in the air and looked around the lobby. "I'll have a porter bring it in."

"Oh no," Benjamin said.

"Sir?"

"I mean I—I'd rather not go to the trouble of bringing it all in. I just have a toothbrush. I can get it myself. If that's all right."

"Of course."

Benjamin reached for the key.

"I'll have a porter show you the room."

"Oh," Benjamin said, withdrawing his hand. "Well actually I'd just as soon find it myself. I just have the toothbrush to carry up and I think I can handle it myself."

"Whatever you say, sir." The man handed him the key.

"Thank you."

Benjamin walked across the lobby and out through the front doors of the hotel. He watched the doorman open the doors of several cars and the taxi that drove up, then he turned around and went back inside. As he passed the clerk he stopped and patted one of the pockets of his coat.

"Got it," he said.

"Sir?"

"The toothbrush. I got the toothbrush all right."

"Oh. Very good, sir."

Agendas, arguments, barriers and fear—by keeping these four things in mind your dialogue will sizzle as well as dazzle. You'll be pulling readers into the heat of every scene. This results in what we call a page turner.

Now let me give you my favorite tools for improving dialogue even more.

6

CRAFT SECRETS FOR SHAPING GREAT DIALOGUE

I like to give nuts and bolts in my workshops, tips that actually work, that have been tested and tried in experience. So this chapter is no theory and all practicality. Here are my eleven best tools for writing dazzling dialogue. They work for me and have for countless of my students, so I think I'm safe in saying they'll work for you, too.

Orchestration

Great dialogue begins before you write a line.

It starts by creating a cast of characters who differ from each other so there is always the possibility of conflict or tension.

Let's take a genuine classic of American literature as an example. I've already used several examples from *The Maltese Falcon* earlier in this book. That's because in my opinion it should replace *The Great Gatsby* on a must-read high school list. What Dashiell Hammett did was nothing less than found a genre, the hard-boiled detective novel.

And he did it by infusing every scene with orchestrated tension that comes out in the dialogue.

The lead character is Sam Spade, a battle-tested gumshoe. How would such a man talk?

He wouldn't mince words. He'd get to the point. If you started talking nonsense, he'd cut you off with a sharp remark.

What kind of characters would you put him in scenes with?

How about Joel Cairo? A diminutive dandy of some European background. Obviously educated and a man of breeding. The opposite of Spade.

Then there is Casper Gutman, the fat man, the master-mind of the quest for the bird. He has money and means, and where Spade's talk is clipped, his is garrulous. Thus we have:

The fat man looked shrewdly at Spade and asked: "You're a close-mouthed man?"

Spade shook his head. "I like to talk."

"Better and better!" the fat man exclaimed. "I distrust a close-mouthed man. He generally picks the wrong time to talk and says the wrong things. Talking's something you can't do judiciously unless you keep in practice." He beamed over his glass. "We'll get along, sir, that we will." He set his glass on the table and held the box of Coronas del Ritz out to Spade. "A cigar, sir."

And then there is the femme fatale, Brigid O'Shaughnessy. What a cool liar she is, a shapeshifter. Even when she's called out by Spade for her lies, she pretends to repent, then lies some more.

"What makes it worth all that money?" he demanded. "You must have some idea, at least be able to guess."

"I haven't the slightest idea."

He directed the scowl at her. "What's it made of?"

"Porcelain or black stone. I don't know. I've never touched it. I've only seen it once, for a few minutes. Floyd showed it to me when we first got hold of it." ...

"You are a liar."

She got up and stood at the end of the table, looking down at him with dark abashed eyes in a pinkening face. "I am a liar," she said. "I have always been a liar."

"Don't brag about it. It's childish." His voice was good-humored. He came out from between table and bench. "Was there any truth at all in that yarn?"

She hung her head. Dampness glistened on her dark lashes. "Some," she whispered.

"How much?"

"Not—not very much."

Throughout the novel the dialogue is tense between all the characters because they are so different from one another.

Here's another example of the power of orchestration. One of the great comedy hits in TV history is *The Office* (derived from the British series of the same name). The show had a large ensemble, and every single character had his or her own unique set of quirks. In each show, therefore, every character could, at any time, be in conflict with any other character. And all of them could be in conflict with the hapless boss, Michael.

Notice something else about this show. The amusing dialogue was never forced. It flowed naturally from the characters, which is what great orchestrated dialogue does.

For your novel:

1. Make a list of your cast. Give each character a one or two line description.

2. Step back and make sure the descriptions are sufficiently different from each other.

3. Give each character one quirk. Make them irritating to at least two other characters.

4. Write a few "practice scenes" pairing two of the characters at random. These are great warm up exercises for your writing, and may generate actual plot ideas and twists.

Flip The Obvious

Every now and then pause in the middle of a dialogue scene. Look at what you've written and ask if any of the dialogue is "obvious." Is it something a reader would expect a character to say?

If so, flip it. Have the character say the exact opposite. What does that show you?

Here's an example:

"I do love you, John," Stella said.

"How much?" John said.

"Oh, don't put me on the spot like that."

"Come on. I want to know."

"You're treating me like a child."

"Be a kid then. How much?"

Stella laughed. "All right. As much as I love pizza. And that's a lot."

Okay, it's not Proust. But let's play with it. Let's flip the obvious:

"I do love you, John," Stella said.

"How much?" John said.

"Enough to barf."

Or:

"I do love you, John," Stella said.

"How much?" John said.

"Oh, don't put me on the spot like that."

"Because I can't stand the sight of you."

Why would John say that? Figure it out. Is he joking? Or is there some other issue there?

Another way to get rid of the obvious is with my dialogue randomizer. Here's how it works.

Pick a scene heavy with dialogue. Count the lines of dialogue on one page.

Now using a random number generator (you can find these by googling "random number generator") select a line of dialogue.

Now, go to your bookshelf—or e-reader—and choose a favorite novel. Go to a random page in that novel. Find the first line of dialogue on that page (or whatever subsequent page dialogue appears on).

Now, insert that line of dialogue in place of the one you selected in your manuscript.

That's what I said.

It will probably be completely outrageous and inexplicable.

Good.

Tweak it. Keep the sense of it, but fit it into your scene. Here's an example from my novel, *Don't Leave Me.* Chuck Samson is a former Navy chaplain who served with a Marine unit in Afghanistan. He's come home to take care of his adult, autistic brother, Stan. In the opening scene a knife-wielding man confronts Chuck and Stan with a knife before driving off. A driver in a sedan arrives a moment after.

"What was that?" the sedan driver yelled. "Was that a knife?"

Stan gripped Chuck's arm. "He had a knife, Chuck. Did you see the knife?"

"I'll call 911," the driver said. He was maybe fifty, short gray hair and glasses.

"Yeah, yeah," Chuck said. He looked to his brother. Stan was trembling. Chuck gently gripped Stan's shoulders. "It's okay now, bud."

"Why did he have a knife, Chuck?"

"I don't know. But he's gone."

"I have to go to work. The new specials are out!"

"We'll get you there. Don't worry. Don't—"

Chuck's phone vibrated. He fished it from his pocket. A private number. "Hello?"

A male voice, whispery, said, "Don't say a word."

"What?"

"You do and you're dead."

"Wait a—"

"She would not like that."

That's fourteen lines. A random number generator gives me the number 5.

Next, I choose one of my favorite novels. Here on the shelf, I pull down *L.A. Requiem* by Robert Crais. Opening it at random, I come to page 204. And I find the first line to be: "Wild things are everywhere." Here is the re-written exchange:

"What was that?" the sedan driver yelled. "Was that a knife?"

Stan gripped Chuck's arm. "He had a knife, Chuck. Did you see the knife?"

"I'll call 911," the driver said. He was maybe fifty, short gray hair and glasses.

"Yeah, yeah," Chuck said. He looked to his brother. Stan was trembling. Chuck gently gripped Stan's shoulders. "It's okay now, bud."

"Wild things are everywhere."

That's a great line for this character!

What if I had chosen another novel? In a different genre? I pull out *I Am Charlotte Simmons* by Tom Wolfe. 216: "Maybe some wine."

"What was that?" the sedan driver yelled. "Was that a knife?"

Stan gripped Chuck's arm. "He had a knife, Chuck. Did you see the knife?"

"I'll call 911," the driver said. He was maybe fifty, short gray hair and glasses.

"Yeah, yeah," Chuck said. He looked to his brother. Stan was trembling. Chuck gently gripped Stan's shoulders. "It's okay now, bud."

"Maybe some wine."

Wow! For my character, Stan, an autistic adult, to say that brings up all sorts of wonderful, new possibilities. But I decided to go with the other line.

This is a hugely fun exercise, especially if you feel tired or bogged down in your writing day.

Subtext

Think of an iceberg.

Now think of Leonardo DiCaprio.

They are both, like good subtext, mostly under the surface of the water.

When you write a scene, your text is above the surface. That's what the reader sees. But underneath you have a huge chunk of unseen ice. Indeed, that is the dangerous part of the iceberg. That's the part that's a mystery.

Most subtext should operate like that. In other words, what's going on in the scene is more than what is seen. See?

Let me give you an example from a great old paperback original, *Don't Cry For Me* by William Campbell Gault (1952):

Spaghetti Neapolitan, we had. With sausage, that means, and ham and mushrooms and onions. And, of course, garlic.

Wine we had, red and cheap.

After the third glass of that, she said, "You could work, you know. You're not so dumb you couldn't find a job."

"What kind?" I asked her. "I can throw a football, though not up to Waterfield or Van Brocklin, not well enough to get paid for it. And I carried a rifle for four years, but who's paying for that now?"

"The same employer," she said. "Though he's moved his plant. You'll be carrying a rifle yet, if you don't get a job, I'll bet."

"What are you saying?" I asked her. "Get in defense work now, get essential?"

"You certainly must loathe the army, the way I've heard you talk about it."

"I also loathe the time clock, and am not a guy to play it cute. Let us not talk of defense work."

"You could run an elevator or drive a truck, I'll bet. Or sell sportswear in some ritzy shop. Even with that nose you have a certain flair."

"Relax, Irish," I said. "Have some more wine. Don't fret about me."

"Somebody has to," she said.

"Nobody has to," I told her. "Nobody ever has."

Can you get a sense of these two just from the dialogue? What their background might be? Their life experience? Their expectations?

You can weave subtext naturally into your dialogue

scenes by knowing things a) the reader doesn't, and/or b) the other character doesn't. What sorts of things might these be?

- Secrets
- Past relationships
- Rich backstory
- Shocking experiences
- Vivid memories
- Fears
- Hopes
- Yearnings

My favorite generator of subtext is the "character web." Take a sheet of blank paper (I find this much easier to do with pen and paper) and write down the names of all the major characters in a rough circle.

Next, draw a line from one character to another. Ask: what is their relationship? Are they complete strangers? What if there was some sort of past connection? Is this connection known to them? Or only to one? Or none?

Play awhile with that connection and see what develops. If you come up with something interesting, it will provide plenty of subtext for your scenes with those two characters. It will also give you plot material, too.

Now, repeat this with two other characters.

And again.

Do this as many times as you want with as many character relationships as you want. Of course, all the characters won't have connections with each other. But this way you'll brainstorm into some great possibilities for your novel.

And your dialogue will pulse with subtext as a result.

The Cheap Champagne Method

Let the dialogue flow. Pop open your talk bottle and pour it out on the page.

And do it without quote marks, attributions or actions beats.

What you're doing is letting the characters improvise a scene for you.

Know and accept the fact that you will cut much of this dialogue. That's fine. It's not going to take you all that long to write, plus it is good writing practice.

But in the midst of it all you'll find actual lines, plot twists, points of conflict and other fictional matter you couldn't find any other way.

Your writer's mind—which is a basement full of non-union imagination workers who happily labor without coffee breaks, donuts, sleep, or management concessions—will get into the game and send you cool stuff.

James Frey even lets it flow in his novel *Bright Shiny Morning:*

What's up, Larry?

What's up, Ricardo?

You know the rules, right?

Yeah.

You gotta be outta the bathroom by the time we open.

I know.

Your stuff was in there this morning. You were nowhere to be found.

I got mugged.

What?

Not really mugged, because I got nothing to steal. But I got kicked in the head this morning and I got knocked out.

Seriously?

Yeah.

Who knows? Maybe Frey did this page after page when drafting and wrote most of the book that way.

A lot of writing teachers advocate "morning pages" or "writing practice," which is basically keeping the words going for five, ten minutes at a time without the inner editor interfering.

Why not turn that writing practice into let-it-flow dialogue that you may actually end up using?

Parent, Adult, Child

Back in the 60s a book was published called *Games People Play* by Dr. Eric Berne. It took off, becoming a pop psychology sensation. I have no idea whether "transactional analysis" has or had any validity. I never read the book cover to cover.

But one idea therein became an indispensable tool for my dialogue. I was turned onto the idea by Jack Bickham's *Writing Fiction That Sells* (1989).

Put simply, the idea in transactional analysis is that we tend to relate to each other by the roles we see ourselves in. These roles fall into one of three categories:

Parent: This is the role of full authority. The Parent can

lay down the law and enforce it. The Parent is the "final word." If there's an argument, the Parent pulls rank. "My way or the highway" was coined by a Parent.

Adult: This is the even-minded, even-tempered role. The Adult says, "Let's be objective about this." Balanced, rational, analytical. The sort of person you want in charge in a crisis.

Child: Emotional, irrational, selfish, whiny, trusting, innocent, tantrum-throwing, pouting.

Now, isn't it easy to see how this can work to bring out conflict in dialogue? If you have characters operating in different roles, or in the same role with opposite agendas, the tension is automatic. The one exchange to be careful with is the Adult to Adult conversation. You will need to add some tension to that scene, usually via the fear factor and barriers (see the previous chapter).

Let's look at a typical scene from an early *Law & Order* episode. There's always a scene in the police interview room, where the two detectives have brought in a suspect. They play a game of good cop/bad cop, and the suspect arrogantly mocks the proceedings.

In that case, the bad cop is playing the Parent. He is yelling, demanding, threatening.

The good cop is the Adult in the room. He tells bad cop to calm down. Go get some coffee. I'll take it from here.

And the suspect is, of course, the child. Ha ha, big game we're playing. I can act like a jerk and you can't do anything about it.

So any transaction between the characters is fraught with conflict.

Here is a simple but powerful exercise. Just before you

start writing a scene, jot down what role the characters think they're playing. Figure out the natural points of conflict.

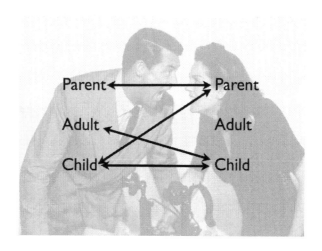

Whatever it is, you'll immediately have a stronger scene going.

Note, during a scene characters can change roles for strategic purposes. If an Adult isn't getting his way, he can become a Parent for a while, or a Child.

Using the Parent-Adult-Child matrix is flexible and doesn't take much time. But the benefits to your dialogue will be enormous.

Curving the Language

"Everything I learned about comedy writing I learned from Danny Simon," Woody Allen has said (as quoted in *Woody Allen* by Eric Lax). Indeed, Allen and Neil Simon both credit

Neil's older brother for teaching them to write successful comedy.

Clearly, Danny Simon was a man who knew what he was doing in the area of narrative comedy. He made his bones in the golden age of TV comedy, on shows like *Make Room for Daddy* and Sid Caesar's *Show of Shows*.

He taught a legendary comedy writing class in L.A. for many years before his death in 2005.

I took the class. It was a great experience, and since I took copious notes, I was able to preserve his comedy writing principles for the world. I put them into a booklet called *How To Write Comedy: The Danny Simon Notes*. I mention this for two reasons.

First, comedy is the hardest form of fiction there is. If you practice it, your overall writing (especially dialogue) will only get better.

Second, Danny had a little exercise he called "curving the language." Here's what he meant. The joke writers on the old *Tonight Show* with Johnny Carson were trying to come up with something about the Macy's Thanksgiving Day parade. That's the one with the big balloons of cartoon characters and the like. So the writers first laid out a premise for the joke.

At the Macy's parade, a big balloon got loose and popped on a building.

That's not funny. Yet. Now they "curved the language." They played with the basic skeleton. Next came:

At the Macy's parade, the Snoopy balloon got loose and popped on the Chrysler building.

Better, but still not a joke worthy of Carson. Finally, they finished with:

There was a tragedy at the Macy's Thanksgiving Day parade. The Snoopy balloon got loose ... and was neutered by the Chrysler building.

So what does this mean for you, dialogue maker? It means that you can create memorable lines for your characters with a little curving. You write out the lines as they come to you, but later go back and find some that you can pump up. Let's say you were writing *The Godfather* (and as long as we're saying that, you got to cash all the checks, too), and Michael Corleone has come to Las Vegas to tell the older, more established Moe Green that the Corleone family is buying out his interest in the casinos.

Moe Green is outraged. What does he say in response? At first, you might write it like this:

"I'm Moe Green! I was running this place when you were in high school!"

Not striking enough. So you tweak it:

"I'm Moe Green! I made my bones when you were in high school!"

A little better. But we can do more with it. In the movie the line is:

"I'm Moe Green! I made my bones when you were going out with cheerleaders!"

Off The Nose

There's a derogatory term out of Hollywood: On-the-nose dialogue. This refers to an unsurprising and direct response to what is being said, as in:

"Let's go to the store, Al."

"Okay, Bill, that's a fine idea."

"I always have fine ideas, don't I?"

"Not always. I remember the time you wanted to build a rocket."

"That was a hoot, building that rocket."

"Yes, rocket building is always a hoot."

"Does anyone say 'hoot' anymore?"

"We certainly do!"

"Yes, I guess that's true! We just did, didn't we?"

"We sure did."

"I forgot, are you Al or Bill?"

"Gee, I forgot, too. Let's go back to the top of this dialogue and find out."

"Fine idea! Let's!"

It's not that we don't need to do this sometimes in dialogue. After all, if there was never any on-the-nose talk, we'd all be confused about what was going on.

But mix in a healthy dose of the "side-step" in your dialogue, and instantly the interest level will pick up.

For instance:

"Let's go to the store, Al."
  "Your wife called me yesterday."

See that? A totally off-kilter response. The reader has a subconscious nudge, asking why did he say that? What's the meaning behind it?

In other words, more interest.

"Let's go to the store, Al."
  "Why don't you shut your fat face?"

Any conflict there? I think so.

"Let's go to the store, Al."
  "Okay, Bill, that's a fine idea."
  "Why aren't you wearing pants?"

A total surprise. This is the dialogue equivalent of the old Raymond Chandler suggestion that, if a scene is dull, you just bring in a guy with a gun.

You can easily come up with ideas for what I call "side-steps" just by going through your dialogue, finding the dull exchanges, and figuring out something else.

Compression

Unless there is a reason for a character to be running off at the mouth, dialogue is usually best when it is compressed. That is, cut it down so it is like the mutton, lettuce and tomato sandwich in *The Princess Bride:* nice and lean.

Consider the following:

"My, it's a wonderful day to be walking in the park, isn't it?"

"I wish you would not talk like everything is so rosy all the time."

"Do I? Do I do that? I assure you it's not intentional! I simply see the glass as half full."

"Do you want to know what I think? I think you yourself are half full. Half full of it, that is."

Now let's do some compression.

"Nice day for the park."

"Don't talk like everything's rosy all the time."

"I see the glass as half full."

"I think you're half full. Of it."

Notice that you can often cut words at the beginning of the lines. Often we let our own speech begin with words like *Well, Like, Yes, No.* Or we'll offer an on-the-nose starter that is based on what the previous speaker said:

"You're always doing that."

"I am? I don't mean to."

That *"I am?"* is fluff. It's not needed. Better is:

"You're always doing that."
  "I don't mean to."

* * *

"You're always doing that."
  "Yes. You're right. But I am an optimist."

Better:

"You're always doing that."
  "I'm an optimist."

Simply cutting those fluff words at the beginning will help with compression. Again, if you have a reason for a character to use fluff words, by all means use them. Let's go back to the opening of *The Last Coyote* by Michael Connelly:

"Any thoughts that you'd like to start with?"
  "Thoughts on what?"
  "Well, on anything. On the incident."
  "Oh, the incident. Yes, I have some thoughts."

We learn that this is a psychologist talking to Detective Harry Bosch. She is treading lightly, so uses *Well* as a warm up. And Bosch is sarcastic, so his last line uses repetition as a weapon.

In other words, Connelly had a reason for rendering the dialogue with some fluff.

Unless you have an equally good reason, don't do it.

Try this with one of your dialogue scenes. Make a copy of it, then try cutting the dialogue to the bone. Compare the two versions and incorporate the cuts that work. This exercise is virtually guaranteed to dazzle up your dialogue.

Don't Forget About Silence

A powerful variation on the sidestep is silence. It is often the best choice, no matter what words you might come up with. Hemingway was a master at this. Consider this excerpt from his short story "Hills Like White Elephants." A man and a woman are having a drink at a train station in Spain. The man speaks:

> "Should we have another drink?"
>
> "All right."
>
> The warm wind blew the bead curtain against the table.
>
> "The beer's nice and cool," the man said.
>
> "It's lovely," the girl said.
>
> "It's really an awfully simple operation, Jig," the man said. "It's not really an operation at all."
>
> The girl looked at the ground the table legs rested on.
>
> "I know you wouldn't mind it, Jig. It's really not anything. It's just to let the air in."
>
> The girl did not say anything.

In this story, the man is trying to convince the girl to have an abortion (a word that does not appear anywhere in the text). Her silence is reaction enough.

By using a combination of sidestep, silence and action, Hemingway gets the point across through a brief, compelling exchange. He uses the same technique in this well-known scene between mother and son in the story "Soldier's Home":

> "God has some work for everyone to do," his mother said. "There can be no idle hands in His Kingdom."
>
> "I'm not in His Kingdom," Krebs said.
>
> "We are all of us in His Kingdom."
>
> Krebs felt embarrassed and resentful as always.
>
> "I've worried about you so much, Harold," his mother went on. "I know the temptations you must have been exposed to. I know how weak men are. I know what your own dear grandfather, my own father, told us about the Civil War and I have prayed for you. I pray for you all day long, Harold."
>
> Krebs looked at the bacon fat hardening on the plate.

Silence and bacon fat hardening. We don't need anything else to catch the mood of the scene. What are your characters feeling while exchanging dialogue? Try expressing it with the sound of silence.

Controlling Pace Through Dialogue

Simple rule of thumb: If you want to slow down the pace of your story, you increase the description between the dialogue and decrease the white space on the page.

If you need to speed things up, decrease the description and increase the white space.

Here's a bit of dialogue from one of the masters of clipped prose, Ken Bruen, in *The Guards:*

Went to the florist's. It was the same girl who'd sold me the roses. She said,
  "I remember you."
  "Right."
  "Did they work?"
  "What?"
  "The roses, for your lady?"
  "Good question."
  "Ah ... that's a pity. You're going to try again?"
  "Not exactly."
  "Oh?"
  "I need a wreath."
  A look of horror, then,
  "Did she die?"
  "No ... no, somebody else. A friend."
  "I am sorry."

It's fast. There's a huge amount of white space and no pausing for descriptive elements. The strategy here is to move the outer story along at a brisk pace.

Now let's take that same dialogue and make an entirely different scene out of it. With apologies to Ken Bruen:

  "I remember you."
  "Right," I said. I felt like a jerk. The last time I was here I acted like one, and now here I was again asking her to go through the same routine.
  "Did they work?" she asked.

"What?"

"The roses, for your lady?"

She had to ask, didn't she? Had to bring it all up again. For half a second I thought about the lady who was not my lady anymore. It was like somebody sticking thorns in my brain.

"Good question," I said. I am really quite eloquent in situations like this.

"Ah ... that's a pity. You're going to try again?"

"Not exactly," I said, and was about to be a jerk to her again, but I kept the words in the back of my throat.

"Oh?" she said.

"I need a wreath," I said.

A look of horror, then,

"Did she die?"

"No ... no, somebody else. A friend."

"I am sorry."

No you're not, but you have to say it and I'll just let it pass this time. Just get me the wreath and let me out of here. I need a drink, and the sooner the better.

Obvious differences. What the first example gave us was speed and subtext. We are left to fill in the blanks of what's going on ourselves. That's a definite strategy, one that Bruen uses skillfully.

The second example would be used when the writer wants to go deeper than subtext and enlarge the inner life of the character.

What strategy you use at any given time in your dialogue is up to you, of course. Just be intentional about it.

Use dialogue like an orchestra leader's baton. Slow down, speed up, make music.

Gems and Spice

Every now and then you want a bit of dialogue to sparkle, to spice up a scene. Anything that moves a reader emotionally, or gives them an added bit of pleasure. Here is a bit from the script of what many people consider the greatest film ever made, *Citizen Kane*. The script was co-written by Orson Welles and Herman J. Mankiewicz. Welles himself gave Mankiewicz credit for the following:

THOMPSON
Well, Mr. Bernstein, you were with Mr. Kane from the very beginning -

BERNSTEIN
From before the beginning, young fellow. And now it's after the end.
(turns to Thompson)
Anything you want to know about him, about the paper—

THOMPSON
We thought maybe, if we can find out what he meant by that last word - as he was dying -

BERNSTEIN
That Rosebud? Maybe some girl? There were a lot of them back in the early days, and -

THOMPSON
Not some girl he knew casually and then remembered after
fifty years, on his death bed -

BERNSTEIN
You're pretty young, Mr. Thompson. A fellow will
remember things you wouldn't think he'd remember. You
take me. One day, back in 1896, I was crossing over to Jersey
on a ferry and as we pulled out, there was another
ferry pulling in -
(slowly)
- and on it, there was a girl waiting to get off. A white dress
she had on, and she was carrying a white parasol. And I
only saw her for one second and she didn't see me at all. But
I'll bet a month hasn't gone by since that I haven't thought
of that girl.
(triumphantly)
See what I mean?
(smiles)
Well, so what are you doing about this "Rosebud," Mr.
Thompson?

That bit about the girl with the parasol is one of the
most talked about moments in the entire film. It's a gem. It
carries a rich, emotional appeal. And it also subtly rein-
forces the theme that money is not what people truly want
in life.

Now here's some spice. This is dialogue written by the
great Raymond Chandler for the film *Double Indemnity*. In
this early scene, Walter Neff, crack insurance salesman, has
paid a call on a client, Dietrichson. But the man isn't home.

His wife, Phyllis, is. And as the scene goes along we see Neff making subtle verbal suggestions. Finally, Phyllis calls him on it:

PHYLLIS
Mr. Neff, why don't you drop by tomorrow evening about eight-thirty. He'll be in then.

NEFF
Who?

PHYLLIS
My husband. You were anxious to talk to him weren't you?

NEFF
Sure, only I'm getting over it a little. If you know what I mean.

PHYLLIS
There's a speed limit in this state, Mr. Neff. Forty-five miles an hour.

NEFF
How fast was I going, officer?

PHYLLIS
I'd say about ninety.

NEFF
Suppose you get down off your motorcycle and give me a ticket.

PHYLLIS
Suppose I let you off with a warning this time.

NEFF
Suppose it doesn't take.

PHYLLIS
Suppose I have to whack you over the knuckles.

NEFF
Suppose I bust out crying and put my head on your shoulder.

PHYLLIS
Suppose you try putting it on my husband's shoulder.

NEFF
That tears it.

Neff takes his hat and briefcase.

NEFF
Eight-thirty tomorrow evening then, Mrs. Dietrichson.

PHYLLIS
That's what I suggested.

NEFF
Will you be here, too?

PHYLLIS

I guess so. I usually am.

NEFF
Same chair, same perfume, same anklet?

PHYLLIS
(Opening the door)
I wonder if I know what you mean.

NEFF
I wonder if you wonder.

Now that is dialogue mastery. It is perfect for the tone of the story, and stylized in the manner of the time.

TOP TEN DIALOGUE ISSUES

In this section I present the treatment of several issues that come up when writing dialogue. You don't have to read all this word for word. Rather, use this as a reference and refer to it as needed. The subjects are:

1. Punctuation
2. Attributions, Adverbs, Action Tags
3. Dialects
4. Backstory
5. Inner Dialogue
6. Experimental
7. Cursing
8. Thematic Dialogue
9. Comic Relief
10. Period Dialogue

1. PUNCTUATION

The rules for punctuation in dialogue need to become second nature. A skilled editor or reader will notice aberrations. That may not make them reject a book, but it is an unnecessary speed bump.

Here are the rules:

Punctuation goes inside the close quote

"Where are we going?" he asked.

"That's a nice dress," she said.

NOT: "Where are we going"? he asked.

And there's always punctuation

NOT: "That's a nice dress" she said.

The punctuation marks for dialogue are:

Comma.
Period.
Question mark.
Exclamation point.
Em-dash.
Ellipsis.

Never capitalize the pronoun when it's a dialogue attribution

"Get out of this house!" he said.
    NOT: "Get out of this house!" He said.

But do capitalize when it's an action beat

"Get out of this house!" He picked up the gun.
    NOT: "Get out of this house!" he picked up the gun.

Put a comma after an attribution when it comes at the beginning

Mary said, "I wish you would go away and never return."

If there are two or more sentences, and you need a speaker attribution, put it before or after the first complete phrase

Morton said, "Now let me tell you a thing or two. I am not going to stand for this. Not ever."

"Now let me tell you a thing or two," Morton said. "I am not going to stand for this. Not ever."

NOT: "Now let me tell you a thing or two. I am not going to stand for this. Not ever," Morton said.

Put a comma after an attribution when it comes in the middle of a sentence

Sometimes, for variation, you'll want to put the speaker attribution in the middle of a complete sentence, as opposed to the beginning or the end. In that case, a comma goes after it and you don't capitalize the next word:

"I wish you would go away," Mary said, "and never return."

Quotation marks are for spoken words only

NOT: "What am I going to do?" she thought.

Render thoughts either in italics:

What am I going to do?

Or without:

What am I going to do? she thought.

[Note: When you put thoughts in italics (though this is less fashionable these days) you don't need to tell us *she thought*. That's understood. If you don't use italics, some authors like to put in the thought attribution (as in the above example). Others don't bother, letting the readers figure it out from the context. You can also use an action beat: **She walked into the room. What am I going to do?** In this case you don't need **she thought** because it's clear she is doing the thinking]

If your character is recalling something that was said, should that be put in quote marks? No. Use italics instead:

He thought back to what Monica had said. *I don't love you anymore.* And the way she said it! Like a vampire with empty eyes.

If a character is quoting another character, put the interior quote between single quote marks (apostrophes)

"When John came up to me, he said, 'I don't like what you're doing.' And then I laughed at him."

"Oh, that's just Frank. He's always saying, 'I'm the king of the world.'"

No semi-colons, ever, in dialogue

People don't talk like college essays, even when they sound like it.

Which means don't ever use a semi-colon in dialogue.

Never this: "I don't believe that's the proper course of action; if I did, I would say so."

The semi-colon is a burp, a hiccup. It's a drunk staggering out of the saloon at 2 a.m., grabbing your lapels on the way and asking you to listen to one more story. I would advise you never to use them even in narrative portions of your novel. As Kurt Vonnegut once said, "Here is a lesson in creative writing. First rule: Do not use semicolons. They are transvestite hermaphrodites representing absolutely nothing. All they do is show you've been to college."

In non-fiction, semi-colons are fine; they set off thoughts in a way that aids thinking and analysis.

But fiction is about emotion. We don't want readers to feel like they're reading a textbook. Especially when your characters are speaking.

Use exclamation points sparingly!

The exclamation point is a loud party-goer, demanding attention. Overdone, it can be annoying. Be judicious. Not:

"Let's go!"

"Okay!"

"But watch out for the snakes!"

"I hate snakes!"

"That's okay! So did Indiana Jones!"

Blech. If you want to show over-enthusiasm here, the first two would suffice:

"Let's go!"

"Okay!"

"But watch out for the snakes."

"I hate snakes."

"That's okay. So did Indiana Jones."

Paragraph breaks in a monologue

When one character is making a speech, and you want to break up the paragraphs, the proper punctuation is to end a paragraph *without* closing the quote, and then begin the next *with* the quote mark. Like this:

"And so we decided to go to Pennsylvania. It was crazy, the five of us stuffed into a Volkswagen bug. But what did we care? We were young, we were invincible. We were going to take on the whole world! And we didn't care who knew it. We didn't care if we got stopped by the cops. We had a handgun in the glove compartment, and maybe we'd have to use it. We just did not care, can you believe it? We just did not care.

"Then Molly decided she was going to opt out. She made me stop at a gas station, and that's where the whole thing started to go south. It was about ten at night and we were just screaming at each other. Tim and Brick tried to get between me and Molly, but I kept pushing them away. I could do that back then. I had the strength to do it."

He got a far off look. I waited for him to go on.

"Finally Molly just ran off. We never saw her again. Ever."

Johnny took a deep breath, closed his eyes.

I will say that this method, while traditional and perfectly valid, seems out of style today. More often you'll see the breaks come via reaction beats:

"And so we decided to go to Pennsylvania. It was crazy,

the five of us stuffed into a Volkswagen bug. But what did we care? We were young, we were invincible. We were going to take on the whole world! And we didn't care who knew it. We didn't care if we got stopped by the cops. We had a handgun in the glove compartment, and maybe we'd have to use it. We just did not care, can you believe it? We just did not care."

Johnny put the hammer down and ran his fingers through his hair.

"Then Molly decided she was going to opt out. She made me stop at a gas station, and that's where the whole thing started to go south. It was about ten at night and we were just screaming at each other. Tim and Brick tried to get between me and Molly, but I kept pushing them away. I could do that back then. I had the strength to do it."

He got a far off look. I waited for him to go on.

"Finally Molly just ran off. We never saw her again. Ever."

Johnny took a deep breath, closed his eyes.

No punctuation or attributions after an em-dash, except the close quote

The proper form for an interruption is this:

"I'm telling you, we can't go in there. It's just too—"
"Shut up! We're going."

There is no punctuation mark after the em-dash except the close quote.

And don't do this:

"I'm telling you, we can't go in there. It's just too—" she
said.

"Shut up! We're going."

An attribution never goes after the em-dash. If it's
unclear who is speaking, put the *said* or action beat *before*
the em-dash:

She said, "I'm telling you we can't go in there. It's just
too—"

OR

She slammed her purse on the table. "We can't go in
there. It's just too—"

Self-interruptions

On occasion, a character stops talking on his own because
some form of action pops in, as in this example from Hugh
Howey's *Wool:*

"So you're saying—" He rubbed his chin and thought this
through. "You're saying that someone wiped out our
history to stop us from repeating it?"

There's a subtle wrinkle here suggested by the *Chicago
Manual of Style*. When there is no pause in the statement
(and thus, no real interruption) but there is a simultaneous
action, you render it in the following manner:

So you're saying" —he rubbed his chin— "that someone wiped out our history to stop us from repeating it?"

If you want the character's voice to trail off, use the ellipsis, and don't tell us his voice has trailed off.

NOT: "So you're saying ..." He let his voice trail off.

That's redundant. The ellipsis tells us the voice trailed off. Just move right along with an action beat or another character speaking:

"So you're saying ..." He looked at his shoes.

OR

"So you're saying ..."

"What? What am I saying?"

[Note that there is a space between the last word of the dialogue and the first dot of the ellipsis, but not between the last dot and the close quote.]

2. ATTRIBUTIONS, ADVERBS, ACTION TAGS

"So what's the deal on dialogue attributions?" the young writer asked.

"I'll tell you," said the wise old writer. "It's not complicated, but it's important."

"I'm ready to listen!" the young writer asseverated.

The wise old writer slapped him. "Don't ever asseverate anything again. Just listen."

Make said your default

An attribution is there to let the reader know who is speaking. The simple *said* does that and then politely leaves. Some writers, under the erroneous impression that *said* is not creative enough, will strain to find ways not to use it.

This is almost always a mistake.

Readers don't really notice *said*, even as it serves its purpose. Any substitute word causes the readers to do a little more work (more on that below.)

On the flip side, it's possible to use *said* in an abusive fashion. This is done sometimes in hard-boiled fiction, like this:

"Open the door," Jake said.
 "It's open," Sam said.
 "You don't lock your door?" Jake said.
 "Not on Tuesdays," Sam said.
 "That's weird," Jake said.
 "Weird is in this year," Sam said.

In this case, *said* is forced on the readers for no reason. It feels like you're getting tapped on the head with a rubber hammer with every line of dialogue. So leave out the attribution altogether when it's obvious who is speaking.

"Open the door," Jake said.
 "It's open," Sam said.
 "You don't lock your door?"
 "Not on Tuesdays."
 "That's weird."
 "Weird is in this year."

Should you use 'asked'? he asked

There are some teachers who say you should never use *asked* after a question mark. It's redundant, they say.

I find that a bit too picky. I use *said* after a question mark, but also *asked* sometimes, for variety. I have no rule about it. I use what sounds right at the time.

No one has complained yet.

Use alternatives only if absolutely necessary

On occasion, you may need to find a substitute word. *Whispered,* for example.

What about *growled? Barked? Spat? Expostulated?*

Be careful. Almost always, the tone of the scene and the words of the character should tell the reader how the words are being spoken. Instead of using a thesaurus, work harder at making the words and the action more vivid. Let's not see this:

> "Put that down!" Charles shouted with emphasis.
>
> "But it belongs to me!" Oswald declared.
>
> "Put that down," Charles repeated, a bit more sedately but still with insistence.
>
> "You are such an insistent type," said Oswald bitterly.

Ouch. And *sedately? Bitterly?* That brings us to:

Kill most adverbs, but have mercy on some

I'm not the Terminator on this one. I don't go out on a mission to kill all adverbs and never stop until every one is dead. I do think it's best to let the dialogue itself, and surrounding action, make clear how something is said.

But on occasion, if it's the most economical way to indicate something, I may use an adverb. Even though writing sticklers may feel their knickers getting in a twist over adverbs, I write for readers. Most readers don't care about the occasional adverb. Nor do they wear knickers.

Occasionally put 'said' in the middle

Every now and then, just to mix things up, put *said* in the middle of dialogue. Put it in the first natural spot.

"I think I'd better leave," Millicent said, "before I lose my temper."

If one character uses the name of the other character, for emphasis, you can break up the dialogue this way:

"Rocky," Mickey said, "this is the biggest fight of your life, especially considering you're now seventy years old."

Use action beats for variety, but not exclusively

Because dialogue is a form of action, we can utilize the physical to assist the verbal. This is called the *action tag.*

The action tag offers a character's physical movements instead of *said*, such as in Lisa Samson's *Women's Intuition:*

Marsha shoved her music into a satchel. "She's on a no-sugar kick now anyway, Father."

He turned to me with surprise. "You don't say? How come?"

The action tag can follow the line as well:

"Come along, dear." Harriet spun toward the door.

Warning: this is *not* to be done every time in place of

said. Some writers have attempted to write entire novels without once giving an attribution. But the problem is this: every time there's an action, even an innocuous one, the reader forms a picture. Too much of this becomes labor, because the reader's mind is asking for the significance of the picture. The reading experience begins to feel like a series of speed bumps on a road.

> John crossed his legs. "So what are you going to do about it?"
>
> Marsha tapped her finger on the table. "I haven't decided."
>
> John sighed. "Think about it."
>
> Marsha reached for her drink. "I can't think."
>
> John scratched his nose.
>
> "This place is creepy." Marsha looked around the restaurant.
>
> John cleared his throat. "Perhaps we shouldn't have come here."

See what I mean? Use an action tag only for variety, never exclusively. It works best when the action beats also reflect the tone of the scene and what the characters are experiencing, as in this clip from Suzanne Collins's *Mockingjay:*

> I spring up, upsetting a box of a hundred pencils, sending them scattering around the floor.
>
> "What is it?" Gale asks.
>
> "There can't be a cease-fire." I lean down, fumbling as

I shove the sticks of dark gray graphite back into the box. "We can't go back."

"I know." Gale sweeps up a handful of pencils and taps them on the floor into perfect alignment.

"Whatever reason Peeta had for saying those things, he's wrong." The stupid sticks won't go in the box and I snap several in my frustration.

"I know. Give it here. You're breaking them to bits."

He pulls the box from my hands and refills it with swift, concise motions.

"He doesn't know what they did to Twelve. If he could've seen what was on the ground—" I start.

"Katniss, I'm not arguing. If I could hit a button and kill every living soul working for the Capitol, I would do it. Without hesitation." He slides the last pencil into the box and flips the lid closed. "The question is, what are you going to do?"

3. DIALECTS

It was universal in the novels of the 19th century to present slave dialect this way. Harriet Beecher Stowe's *The Minister's Wooing* (1859), for example, has a domestic sounding like this:

"Dat ar' chile gwin' to be spiled, 'cauе dyе's allers a-pickin' at him; he's well enough, on'y let him alone."

Heavy use of dialect is frowned upon these days. Which means, readers frown when they read it, while editors and agents scowl.

Which means use it sparingly and only for a strategic purpose.

This issue is almost exclusively a matter of use in historical fiction. The author wants the reader to know that a character speaks in period dialect, yet doesn't want to make it difficult to read. The answer is to give the readers just a taste of the dialect, then pull back and only hint at it from time to time.

Liz Curtis Higgs does this masterfully in *Thorn in My Heart,* a novel set in 18th century Scotland. In this scene a character named Jamie is on horseback, and a bit lost. He comes to a cottage. A shepherd lives there and comes out to greet him.

"D'ye ken whaur ye're goin', lad?"

Jamie waved vaguely toward the moors. "East to New Galloway, then south along the banks of the Ken."

The older man appraised horse and rider, eyebrows arched. "Not a path the *gentrice* usually favor."

Jamie only shrugged in agreement, hoping to discourage any further questions.

"Name's Gordie Briggs," the shepherd offered, jerking his head toward the cottage. "Join me for a bit o' supper? 'Tis naught but broth and barley, hardly what ye're used to eatin', but—"

That first line is pure dialect. The reader is clued in that this is a man with a heavy Scottish brogue. Yes, there's some work to be done, but that's okay in small bursts. With that initial sound in the reader's mind now, Higgs does much less of the dialect from that point on. Only the occasional word as a reminder.

So here are the guidelines:

1. Decide if dialect is absolutely needed in a scene.

2. If so, go ahead and use it in the first spoken line.

3. Use it sparingly after that, only as a reminder to readers of the voice.

4. BACKSTORY

Sometimes you'll want a character to reveal backstory (character history or other information that occurred prior to the novel's beginning). The following example is from *Big Red's Daughter*, a 1953 novel by John P. McPartland. The villain, Buddy Brown, is drunk. The protagonist, Jim Work, takes Buddy into a diner for coffee. At this point in the novel, the reader thinks Buddy is simply a sociopath.

"Now what's the deal?" I asked him when the waitress turned away.

He looked down at his cup and then raised his head slowly, looking beyond me.

"I was hunted once, when I was a kid in New York," he said.

I waited.

"That was ten years ago. I was fifteen then." He sounded almost sober now, his whispering voice slurred some of the words, but what he was talking about was so real to him that his drunkenness slipped away from him like a heavy, smothering cloak that he had pushed back for a little while.

"Three of us caught the girl at the edge of Central Park. She was with another girl, but we just wanted the one because her guy was the wheel with a big gang down the street. We held her skirt up over her arms and head so she couldn't do nothing but yell, and then we beat her up a little and ran away. We were all laughing when we did it because we were high on sticks, but after a while the sticks wore off.

"We were just punks. We didn't have any loot and we all lived with our folks. Next day we were afraid to go to school or be seen on the street. We knew what was going to happen. The wheel and his gang got Lee—that was one of my friends— at his house. They gave him the business while his old lady was there and his kid brothers and all. They left him alive and that was all they left him. I don't know what happened to him after that, maybe he died. He had nothing left, nothing. You know?"

He looked across the booth at me, his bruised, pale face a little twisted.

"Mick and me, we run off from home. The boys came to my house and worked over my old man to tell where I was. He didn't know, so they gave him the big schlammin. He's never going to get over it."

The slender, drunken boy was talking in his soft whisper, his eyes far away from mine, talking with a clear earnestness as if he were living it all again.

There's more. But notice how McPartland breaks up the speech with paragraphs and reaction beats. It keeps the long narrative from being block after block of monologue.

5. INNER DIALOGUE

Sometimes, you have to give yourself a good talking to.

In fiction, this is called inner dialogue. It's not exactly the same as an inner monologue. It helps greatly to appreciate the difference.

Inner monologue is the character speaking *within* himself. It's his thoughts made manifest on the page. It's letting the reader in on what's happening inside:

> I will do this thing. I will go into the building and march right down to Mr. Milton's office and tell him what I think of him. I will stand on the chair and tell him I am leaving the company and if he doesn't like it he knows what he can do.

Inner dialogue is the character talking *to* himself, almost as if he had two voices:

> So what should I do? I know what I'll do. I'll walk

right into the building and down to Mr. Milton's office. And what if they try to stop me? Who cares? I don't, but maybe I'd better. I don't want to get detained.

Or maybe I should just forget the whole thing.

Sometimes it's a good choice to take a portion of narrative and turn it into inner dialogue. Here's the narrative:

He wondered if his mother was right. That he was born bad and had just gotten worse over the years. Since he was now a cold-blooded killer, perhaps that meant his character was fixed and could not be changed.

Now, let's switch that to inner dialogue:

Mom was right. You're no good. You were born no good and you've just gotten worse. Cold-blooded killer, that's you. So what? That's the way of this big bad world, and you kill or you get killed. So you're a big man now, you kill, how's it feel? She was right, she was right all along, she knew, knew you from the womb. Well sorry, Mom, you had me and now you can deal with it.

6. EXPERIMENTAL

Experimental fiction is, by its very nature, harder for readers to get into. That's okay if that's your purpose. Many writers don't want to bother with craft conventions. So long as you know the risks and are good with the artistic rewards, fine.

Roddy Doyle, in *The Snapper,* makes up his own rules for dialogue. It's an open question whether this is effective or annoying. It's up to the readers, as always:

— You should've come to us earlier — before, yeh know — an' said you were goin' to get pregnant.

The three of them tried to laugh.

— Then we could've done somethin' abou' it. —
— My God, though.

No one said anything. Then Jimmy Sr. spoke again.

— You're absolutely sure now? Positive?
— Yeah, I am. I done—

— Did, said Veronica.

— I did the test.

— The test? said Jimmy Sr. —Oh. —Did yeh go in by yourself.

— Yeah, said Sharon.

Another form of experimentation is not to use any indication at all when it's dialogue and let the reader figure it out.

Let's go, Billy.

Where?

The docks.

The docks was the place Michael liked to go best.

I don't like them, Michael.

So?

So I don't want to go.

You'll go, Michael said.

They went.

Personally, I think this sort of thing makes readers work too hard. But that's one of the points of experimental fiction, isn't it?

If you know why you're doing it, and you can accept the consequences, have at it.

7. CURSING

I have several novelist friends who write thrillers. Two of them have had moderate, but not breakout, success. Interestingly, both have been urged by their publishing houses to get rid of the F bomb. At least, to scale them back.

Why? Because many readers who have money to spend on books do not like being assaulted by that word. The key word is *assaulted*. As in feeling like you're getting your head hammered by a Floyd Mayweather flurry every few chapters.

I am not laying down a rule. What language you use is up to you. I'm just offering a marketing tip. Major publishers are recognizing that too much "harsh language" is affecting sales.

But, you say, My dialogue is realistic! I can't write about street thugs without abundant F bombs.

Well, *Law & Order,* one of the most successful and realistic shows of all time, managed to do it, week after week. You might consider studying some of the episodes.

Remember, fiction is not pure realism. Fiction is stylized realism for a purpose.

One of your purposes is to attract, and not repel, readers.

I'm not saying you should write:

"Oh fudge," the gangbanger said.

But I am saying you can find ways around the harder words *if you so desire.*

How?

- Make the context so clear that whatever is said conveys the tone and substance you're after.

- Try using actions instead of words. For example, a character might spit or hit instead of curse.

- Go ahead and write out the cursing the first time through. Give it a day, then re-read the scene and see how much of it you can cut.

So ...approach cursing with caution. Personally, I avoid those seven words George Carlin once advised you couldn't say on TV (you can Google that if you want to).

But I know many writers don't have the same hesitation, and that's what a robust First Amendment is all about. If that describes you, feel free to disregard this section and do whatever the ... heck you want.

8. THEMATIC DIALOGUE

Here's an exercise for you that will almost automatically deepen your story through thematic dialogue.

1. State the theme

In a separate document, have a key character state the theme in a page-long speech. Have the character argue for it, justify it, as if presenting it to the public.

One of my favorite movies is *On the Waterfront,* starring Marlon Brando and Eva Marie Saint. It's about an ex-boxer, Terry Malloy, who now works as a strong arm for a waterfront boss.

When the mob murders a potential witness against them, Terry comes into contact with the victim's sister, Edie. Not knowing Terry's complicity in her brother's death, Edie is drawn to Terry, as he is to her.

Edie is the exact opposite of Terry. Educated in a Catholic girls' school, she has a view of life that is far different from Terry's. Whereas Terry believes in "do it to him before he does it to you," Edie believes we are all "a part of everybody else."

The movie is about which philosophy Terry will ultimately accept. And it will be Edie's philosophy after all.

So let's have Edie state her philosophy outright. It might go something like this:

> I believe we are all connected. We are all human and, as John Donne said, no man is an island. What one person does affects a whole array of others. If that were not true, who knows what terrible shape the world would be in? Our task upon this earth is to bear witness to this truth, in every way we can, in every venue we can, with every person we can. Oh, some may call this naive, but unless we're willing to risk it, the world will only get worse. Some may call this hopelessly romantic, but without romance, why would we strive?

2. Put the counterargument in the mouth of another character

Terry Malloy might have said something like this:

> I don't have no education, that stuff's for fruitcakes. What you gotta learn you gotta learn by getting knocked around, and learning how to knock the other guy out. That's education. You do that and you get noticed by the people who can make a difference, you know? The guys who can spend two

hundred melons on a suit anytime they want, and not even think about it. There's those guys, and then there's the rest of us, and if you want to hang around with the right people, you forget all that mushy stuff them teachers want you to know and you deal with your fists. That's what it takes to keep alive, man.

3. Now, turn this into a real argument between the two characters

By putting the theme into a tense conversation, it can come out naturally and without preaching. Here's how that conversation took place in the film, *On The Waterfront*:

EDIE: Were you really a prizefighter?

TERRY: I used to be.

EDIE: How did you get interested in that?

TERRY: I don't know. I had to scrap all my life, I might as well get paid for it. When I was a kid my old man got bumped off. Never mind how. Then they stuck Charley and me in a dump they call a "children's home." Boy, that was some home. Anyhow, I ran away from there and fought in the club smokers and peddled papers and Johnny Friendly bought a piece of me.

EDIE: Bought a piece of you?

TERRY: Yes. I was going pretty good there for a while. And after that ...What do you really care, am I right?

EDIE: Shouldn't everybody care about everybody else?

TERRY: Boy, what a fruitcake you are.

EDIE: I mean, isn't everybody a part of everybody else?

TERRY: And you really believe that drool?

EDIE: Yes, I do.

[Drinks are served]

TERRY: Here we are. One for the lady and for the gent. Here's to the first one, I hope it ain't the last. Go ahead.

[Edie sips]

TERRY: No, not like that. One hook.

[Terry drinks his shot]

TERRY: Wham.

[Edie drinks hers, and is jolted]

EDIE: Wham.

TERRY: You wanna hear my philosophy of life? Do it to him before he does it to you.

EDIE: I never met anyone like you. There's not a spark of sentiment, or romance, or human kindness in your whole body.

TERRY: What good does it do you besides get you in trouble?

EDIE: And when things and people get in your way, you just knock them aside, get rid of them. Is that your idea?

TERRY: Don't look at me when you say that. It wasn't my fault what happened to Joey. Fixing him wasn't my idea.

EDIE: Who said it was?

TERRY: Everybody's putting the needle on me. You and them mugs in the church and Father Barry. I didn't like the way he was looking at me.

EDIE: He was looking at everybody the same way.

TERRY: Oh, yeah? What's with this Father Barry? What's his racket?

EDIE: His racket?

TERRY: Yeah, his racket. Everybody's got a racket.

EDIE: But he's a priest.

TERRY: Are you kiddin'? So what? That don't make no difference.

EDIE: You don't believe anybody, do you?

TERRY: Listen, down here it's every man for himself. It's keeping alive. It's standing in with the right people so you get a little bit of change jingling in your pocket.

EDIE: And if you don't?

TERRY: If you don't? Right down.

EDIE: It's living like an animal.

TERRY: All right. I'd rather live like an animal than end up like ...

EDIE: Like Joey? Are you afraid to mention his name?

Here's a bonus tip:

See Terry's last line? "I'd rather live like an animal ..."

A very cool way to present your theme is this: have the character who is going to change at the end state the *opposite* of the theme at the beginning.

For example, in *The Wizard of Oz,* what's the lesson Dorothy learns? "There's no place like home." Early in Act 1, she argues the opposite. Nobody on the farm is listening to her troubles. She can only talk to Toto, thinking there has to be somewhere they can go to escape all care. "Do you suppose there is such a place, Toto? There must be. It's not a place you can get to by a boat or a train. It's far, far away, behind the moon, beyond the rain—" [Cue song]

How about *It's A Wonderful Life?* George Bailey learns, at the end, that his life right there in the town he grew up in, with all his friends, matters. But in the beginning, when he's a boy, he's arguing the opposite. To live, really live, he must travel. Go on adventures. "I'm going out exploring someday, you watch. And I'm going to have a couple of harems, and maybe three or four wives. Wait and see."

This "arguing the opposite" creates a nice thematic arc for the story.

So in your own novel, once you're set on the theme, have your Lead (or the character who changes) argue the other way sometime in Act 1.

9. COMIC RELIEF

Comic relief via dialogue is one of the great, overlooked uses of fictional talk. When you can seamlessly integrate some light talk within a dramatic context, it is highly pleasing to readers.

In my thriller, *The Whole Truth,* my Lead character arrives at a hospital with an urgent desire to see someone. I put in an obstacle in the form of two elderly volunteers who subtly snipe at each other.

> The hospital was tucked up against the foothills. A three story, sage-green structure with tinted windows. Just inside the front doors, two elderly women sat at a reception desk. They were dressed in blue smocks with yellow tags pinned on that said Volunteer. One of them had sleet colored hair done up in curls. The other had dyed hers a shade of red that did not exist in nature.

They looked surprised and delighted when Steve came in, as if he were the Pony Express riding into the fort.

They fought for the first word. Curls said "May I help—" at the same time Red said "Who are you here to—"

They stopped and looked at each other, half annoyed, half amused, then back at Steve.

And spoke over each other again.

"Let me help you out," Steve said. "I'm looking for a doctor, a certain—"

"Are you hurt?" Curls said.

"Our emergency entrance is around to the side," Red said.

"No, I—"

"Oh, but we just had a shooting," Curls said.

"A colored man," Red added.

"Black, Liv. They don't like to be called colored."

"I always forget." Red shook her head.

Steve said, "I'm trying to locate a certain doctor—"

"We don't do referrals here," Curls said. "But if you—"

Red jumped in: "We have a medical building just down the block if you'll—"

"He didn't ask for a medical building," Curls snapped.

"I know that, but if he's looking for a doctor that would be the place to start."

"Not any doctor," Steve said. "A specific doctor, named Walker C. Phillips."

A sudden silence fell upon the volunteers. Neither seemed eager to tackle that one.

"Is he still practicing?" Steve said.

Red leaned forward and whispered. "Lost his license to practice."

"Terrible tragedy," Curls said, shaking her head.

"He drank," Red added, and gave a tippling motion with her hand.

"When was this?" Steve asked.

"Oh, it's been, what, ten years, at least," Curls said. "His wife left him, you know."

"Ah, no, I did not know that."

The two women nodded.

"Can you tell me, is he still around?"

"Oh, he moved," Red said. "To Tehachapi."

"I thought it was Temecula," Curls said.

"No, Tehachapi."

"He moved where the prison is."

"That's Tehachapi."

"No, it's Temecula."

"Oh no. I have a granddaughter in Temecula."

"That doesn't mean—"

"I would have remembered."

"Excuse me," Steve said. "Maybe there's someone here at the hospital who would know for sure?"

I have received many kind comments on this book over the years, and most of them make mention of these two characters, who appear only here.

Any novel or screenplay can benefit from moments of comic relief. They are fun to write, too. It's a chance to create quirky characters and give them memorable things to say.

And that always makes the reading experience more enjoyable.

10. PERIOD DIALOGUE

You know what drives me crazy? Period dialogue that sounds too contemporary. Phrases that come from our time and are transported back into a medieval thriller.

"That was so cool," Sir Lancelot said.

But I have to admit, I may be in the minority. Most readers today don't have that kind of ear.

In fact, if you are really true to period dialogue, much of it will be incomprehensible. If you're writing a thriller set in Shakespeare's time, you don't want readers stumbling over:

"Zounds," said John Smith, "methinks the prenzie Fortanbleu doth wax grubblingly this freolic night."

So what's the answer? A good rule of thumb is to be as neutral as possible, and sprinkle in a period word every now and then.

And when you do, let the context define the word.

"Quit your boasting! You are wearing us out with your gylpwords!"

I don't know what gylpwords are, technically, but it's easy to get the sense from this line. And that's okay. If readers get an inkling of the meaning they won't go running to the Oxford English Dictionary.

Another tip: for educated and upper class characters, you can avoid contractions, thus:

"I'm going to the tournament, and I'll be ready to fight," Sir Lancelot said.

Better would be:

"I am going to the tournament, and I shall be ready to fight," Sir Lancelot said.

But for the lower classes in certain periods, the language would be somewhat less formal. You can make up your own contractions, as Shakespeare did for the gravedigger in *Hamlet:*

"I' faith, if he be not rotten before he die."

Doing some research is essential. Read books of the period, letters, journals. Pick up the cadences.

Period dialogue is tricky, but extremely satisfying when you've done it well.

ABOUT THE AUTHOR

 JAMES SCOTT BELL is a winner of the International Thriller Writers Award and the #1 bestselling author of books on the craft of fiction. He studied writing with Raymond Carver at the University of California, Santa Barbara, and graduated with honors from the University of Southern California Law Center.

A former trial lawyer, Jim writes full time in his home town of Los Angeles.

For More Information
JamesScottBell.com

WRITING RESOURCES

Here are a few resources for you to continue your writing journey.

First, please take a moment to sign up for my occasional email updates. You'll be the first to know about my book releases and special deals. My emails are short and I won't stuff your mailbox, and you can certainly unsubscribe at any time. In return, you get a free book! CHECK IT OUT.

If you're reading the print version, go to:

JamesScottBell.com

And navigate to the FREE BOOK page.

Online Course

<u>**Writing a Novel They Can't Put Down**</u>

A comprehensive training course in the craft of best-selling fiction. An investment that will pay off for your entire career.

The books below are by me unless otherwise indicated:

Plot & Structure
Write Your Novel From the Middle
Plot & Structure
Super Structure
Conflict & Suspense
How to Write Pulp Fiction

Revision
Revision & Self-Editing
27 Fiction Writing Blunders - And How Not to Make Them
Self-Editing for Fiction Writers (Renni Browne and Dave King)

Dialogue
How to Write Dazzling Dialogue

Style
Voice: The Secret Power of Great Writing
Description (Monica Wood)(print only)

· · ·

Publishing & Career
How to Make a Living as a Writer
Marketing For Writers Who Hate Marketing
The Art of War for Writers
How to Write Short Stories and Use Them to Further Your Writing Career
Self-Publishing Attack!

Writing & the Writing Life
Just Write: Creating Unforgettable Fiction and a Rewarding Writing Life Kindle Edition
The Mental Game of Writing
Writing Fiction for All You're Worth
Fiction Attack!
How to Achieve Your Goals and Dreams
How to Manage the Time of Your Life

Nonfiction
On Writing Well (William Zinsser)
Damn! Why Didn't I Write That? (Marc McCutcheon)

Recommended Writing Blogs
KillZoneBlog.com
TheCreativePenn.com
WriterUnboxed.com
WritersHelpingWriters.net
HelpingWritersBecomeAuthors.com

Printed in Great Britain
by Amazon

53030757R00079